Name

Class

Teacher

Safar Islamic Studies Textbook 2

Part of the Safar Learn about Islam Series

Sixth edition, 2019 (Reprinted, 2021)

First published 2013

Published by

Safar Publications, London, England

www.safarpublications.org

info@safarpublications.org

Edited by

Hasan Ali

Muhammed Ahmed

Designed and illustrated by

Reedwan Iqbal

ISBN 978-1-912437-27-6

A catalogue record for this book is available from the British Library.

Printed in Turkey

Safar

Islamic Studies

Textbook 2

Safar Publications

Edited by

Hasan Ali

Muhammed Ahmed

Designed and illustrated by

Reedwan Iqbal

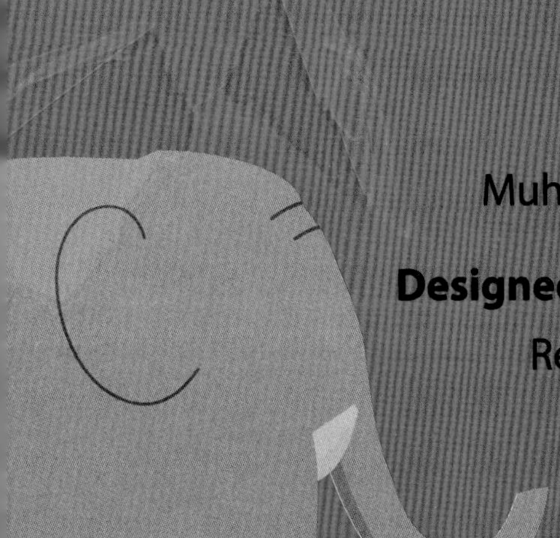

Contents

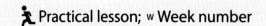

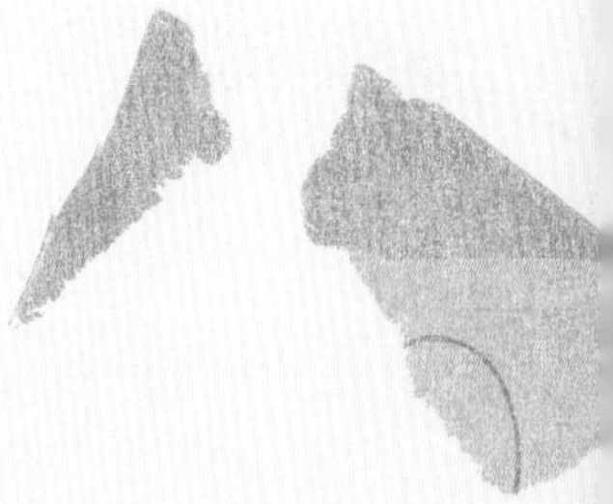

Practical lesson; W Week number

Aqīdah, *Fiqh*, History, *Sīrah*, Personal development

Transliteration key

ء أ إ	’	A light catch in the breath; Qur’ān, *‘Ishā’*
ا	a ā	*Allāhu akbar*, Islām
ب	b	*Bismillāh*
ت	t	*Takbīr*
ث	th	Pronounced as the *th* in thin or thirst; *thawāb*
ج	j	Jannah
ح	ḥ	Tensely breathed *h* sound, produced by a strong expulsion of air from the chest and by narrowing the passage in the depth of the throat; *Ḥaj*
خ	kh	Guttural *ch* as in the Scottish loch with the mouth hollowed to produce a full sound; *ākhirah*
د	d	Pronounced lightly; *du‘ā’*
ذ	dh	Should be pronounced as the *th* in this or that; *Adhān*

ر	r	*Raḥmah*
ز	z	*Zakāh*
س	s	*Sūrah*
ش	sh	*Shahādah*
ص	ṣ	A heavy *s* pronounced with the mouth hollowed to produce a full sound; *Ṣalāh*
ض	ḍ	A heavy *d/dh* pronounced with the mouth hollowed to produce a full sound; Ramaḍān
ط	ṭ	A heavy *t* pronounce with the mouth hollowed to produce a full sound; *shayṭān*
ظ	ẓ	A heavy *dh* pronounced with the mouth hollowed to produce a full sound; *Ẓuhr*
ع	ʿ ʿa ʿi ʿu	Pronounced from the throat, by narrowing the passage in the depth of the throat; *ʿAṣr, ʿIshāʾ, ʿUmrah*
غ	gh	Pronounced with the mouth hollowed to produce a full sound; *ghusl*

ف	f	*Fajr*
ق	q	A guttural *q* sound with the mouth hollowed to produce a full sound; Qur'ān
ك	k	*Kalām*
ل	l	*Labbayk*
م	m	*Mu'min*
ن	n	*Nūr*
و	w ū	*Tawḥīd, wuḍū'*
ه	h	*Hijrah*
ي	y ī	Ubayy, *īman*, Quraysh

Honorifics

سبحانه وتعالى *Subḥānahū wa taʿālā* follows the mention of Allāh. It means, "May He be glorified and exalted."

صلى الله عليه وسلم *Sallallāhu ʿalayhi wa sallam* follows the mention of Prophet Muḥammad. It means, "May Allāh bless him and give him peace."

عليه السلام *ʿAlayhis salām* follows the mention of a prophet or a messenger. It is translated as, "May the peace of Allāh be upon him."

عليهم السلام *'Alayhimus salām* follows the mention of more than one prophet or messenger.

رضي الله عنه *Raḍiyallāhu 'anhu* follows the mention of a male Companion of the Prophet. It means, "May Allāh be pleased with him."

رضي الله عنها *Raḍiyallāhu 'anhā* follows the mention of a female Companion. It means, "May Allāh be pleased with her."

رضي الله عنهم *Raḍiyallāhu 'anhum* follows the mention of more than one Companion It means, "May Allāh be pleased with them."

رحمه الله تعالى *Raḥimahullāh ta'ālā* is follows the mention of a pious person. It means, "May Allāh, the Exalted, have mercy on him."

Honorific titles and forms of address, such as *Sayyidunā, Ummul mu'minīn, Amīrul mu'minīn,* have been omitted in the text. The readers and teachers are encouraged to use these at all occurences.

Preface

In 1998, our first year, we purchased a number of Islamic Studies curricula from across the globe. However, every curriculum came with its own weaknesses – some more than others – but temporarily, we used various parts of different curricula to continue teaching.

For the long-term, we decided to create a comprehensive cross-curriculum, which would be enjoyable for children and make a positive impression on their identity and moral character. Furthermore, it would imbue them with the spirit of traditional Islam while allowing them to live in harmony with the modern world.

By 2002, I had drafted a 50-page syllabus which outlined much of what should be taught. However, the challenge then, was to organise it in an age-appropriate manner and to create a progressive system of learning. For the next few years, various staff members voluntarily created individual lessons and trialled them; their feedback helped us immensely to re-shape the syllabus model.

In 2007, I led a team to further this work, namely Amjad Shaikh, Mohibur Rahman, Shamim Sobur, A. Mushahid Kader, Sofwan Ahmed and Shahid Bukhari. By 2010, we published the first edition: an in-depth yet concise curriculum, which had all core subjects in year-based textbooks. These books also addressed contemporary issues through weekly lessons, covered over a full academic year by building on core knowledge from previous books. A second full colour edition was published in 2013, which was a substantial improvement on the first edition.

Much was improved in the second edition of the series (and subsequent editions), based on feedback from users. The language and content have been further refined, ensuring a higher degree of concision and suitability.

Each textbook comes with a Teacher's Guide (Schemes of Work) and also has a workbook with two tiers of assessment, based on Bloom's Taxonomy of learning objectives. The most unique aspect of this Islamic Studies series is that it is part of a curriculum composed of four interlinking parts. The other three parts being: Tajwīd (Qā'idah, Tajwid and Juz 'Amma); Memorisation (Du'ā's and Sūrahs); and Arabic.

Finally, we thank Allāh سبحانه وتعالى for giving us this opportunity to serve His *dīn* and pray that He makes the work a true success in both worlds for all those who use it. We ask the reader to pray for us and all those who have contributed to this work, both academically and financially.

Your brother in Islam,
Hasan Ali, MA Education (Psychology)
29 April 2014, 28 Jumādal Ākhirah 1435

Note to parents

As a parent, you can play a key role in improving your child's academic attainment as well as forming good manners. Good quality home learning contributes more to a child's intellectual and social development than formal class-based activities. Regularly talking to your child about their learning and helping them through the process, will greatly increase the benefit gained from this series.

It is important that you allocate some time during the week to revise what has been previously covered with your child in class. The amount of time needed for this will vary according to the ability of your child as well as the complexity of the material. This activity is essential in helping you understand your child's progress and development, as well as supporting the child to revise and retain key learning points.

Reading to your child

Reading together not only helps instil confidence in a child but also creates a positive attitude towards learning. Children who read with their families on a regular basis, develop a love of reading that lasts a lifetime. This activity is integral to our teaching methodology.

As parents, you should try your best to:

- Read to your child as often as possible.
- Listen to your child read aloud.
- Ask your child to explain what they have read (or you have read to them) in order to check comprehension. This is an effective method to help strengthen your child's understanding.
- Talk to your child about what has been read. Talking will help your child develop critical thinking skills.
- Set expectations for your child and be clear in articulating these to them.

In class, teachers will not read the stories in the book word for word but rather, deliver the story in a dramatised narrative. This leaves you with a good opportunity to read the story together with your child and discuss the morals and lessons contained within the stories.

Workbook

A workbook is available for each textbook in order to aid your child's learning (according to ability). Please refer to the workbook for further guidance.

Practical checklist

Parents are role models for their children. When children see their parents getting involved in their learning, they tend to be much more enthusiastic about engaging with the content.

Some of the lessons in this textbook have practical aspects which parents can help the child practice at home. Other lessons are best taught by embodying the teachings yourself and being a role model for the child. Below, are lists of such lessons contained in this book as well as a recap of previous lessons.

Lessons: previous

- Using the Muslim greeting: *Assalāmu ʻalaykum*
- Classroom manners.
- Paradise and Hell: explore with your child the concept of accountability for all actions and that good deeds leads to reward and success.
- Manners of using the toilet and keeping clean.
- *Wuḍū'*: help your child practice *wuḍū'* at home.
- The daily *duʻā's* that were taught in Year 1.

Lessons: current

- Deeds: aim to maintain a higher level of consciousness of the consequences of actions, positive or negative. Encourage your child to do good deeds by reminding them that Allāh سبحانه وتعالى will reward them with Jannah.
- *Ṣalāh*: the book contains practical lessons on *Ṣalāh*. You should help your child learn the core actions of performing *Ṣalāh* correctly.

- Cleanliness: ensure your child knows how to clean himself properly and that they take adequate care to keep clothes clean and the body clean from impurities.
- *Wuḍūʾ*: observe your child performing *wuḍūʾ*, ensuring that they perform it properly as laid out in the textbook.
  After *wuḍūʾ*, encourage your child to read the supplication of *wuḍūʾ* loudly.
- *Ghusl*: ensure you child performs *ghusl* regularly, especially on Fridays.
- Good Manners and friendship: discuss the importance of having good manners, as well as teaching them manners and good etiquettes to use in their day-to-day lives. Also, discuss the importance of keeping good friends and good company.

Essential Revision

Core revision

Who am I?

- I am a Muslim.
- My religion is Islām.
- I believe in one Allāh سبحانه وتعالى.
- My Prophet is Muḥammad صلى الله عليه وسلم.
- My holy book is the Qurʾān.

The five pillars of Islām

1. *Shahādah*
2. Ṣalāh
3. Ṣawm (fasting)
4. Zakāh
5. *Ḥajj*

The six articles of faith

1. I believe in Allāh.
2. I believe in angels.
3. I believe in His books.
4. I believe in His messengers.
5. I believe in the Last Day.
6. I believe in destiny (*qadar*).

Wuḍū'

How to do wuḍū':

1. Wash your hands including the wrists three times
2. Rinse your mouth three times
3. Rinse your nose three times
4. Wash your face three times
5. Wash your arms three times
6. Wipe your head, ears and back of the neck once
7. Wash your feet three times

Ghusl

I should have a bath or shower whenever I can. This is called *ghusl* in Arabic. During *ghusl*:

- I need to rinse my mouth and nose with clean water.
- I also need to wash all of my body and all of my hair.

Names and times of *Ṣalāh*

- *Fajr*: before sunrise
- *Ẓuhr*: early afternoon
- *'Aṣr*: late afternoon
- *Maghrib*: after sunset
- *'Ishā'*: night time

Actions of *Ṣalāh*

- *Takbīr*: To raise your hands at the beginning of *Ṣalāh* and say, *"Allāhu akbar"*
- *Qiyām*: To stand during the prayer
- *Rukūʿ*: To bow down
- *Sajdah*: To prostrate
- *Salām*: To turn your head at the end of *Ṣalāh*, once to the right and once to the left

Zakāh and *Ṣadaqah*

- *Zakāh* means to give money to poor people once a year.
- *Sadaqah* also means to give money to the poor (charity). This charity is given by any Muslim at any time. *Sadaqah* does not have to be money. It can be actions, such as smiling or doing something to make someone happy.

Further revision

Allāh

- Allāh سبحانه وتعالى is One and has no family
- Allāh سبحانه وتعالى is All-Seeing
- Allāh سبحانه وتعالى is All-Hearing
- Allāh سبحانه وتعالى is All-Knowing

Angels

Allāh سبحانه وتعالى created many angels out of light. We cannot see angels and they worship Allāh سبحانه وتعالى day and night. The four main angels are:

- Jibrīl عليه السلام: he brought messages to the prophets.
- Mīkā'īl عليه السلام: he brings the rain and food.
- Malakul Mawt عليه السلام: he is the angel of death.
- Isrāfīl عليه السلام: he will blow the trumpet on the Last Day.

Allah's prophets and messengers

Allāh سبحانه وتعالى sent many prophets and messengers to this world. Prophets and messengers teach people about Allāh سبحانه وتعالى. They also teach people to be good and to worship Allāh:

- The first Prophet was Ādam عليه السلام
- The Last Prophet was Muḥammad صلى الله عليه وسلم. There will be no other prophets or messengers sent to this world.

Allāh's books

Allāh سبحانه وتعالى has sent down many books to guide people. The four main books are:

- The Tawrāh
- The Zabūr
- The Injīl
- The Qur'ān: this is the last book sent by Allāh سبحانه وتعالى.

The Day of Judgement

- This is called *Yawmul Qiyāmah* in Arabic.
- On this day, Allāh سبحانه وتعالى will judge everyone. He will decide if people were good or bad.

Paradise and Hell

All Muslims believe in Jannah (Paradise) and Jahannam (Hell). Paradise is very beautiful. You will go to Paradise if you believe in Allāh سبحانه وتعالى, follow Islām, do good actions and listen to your parents.

Bad deeds can lead to punishment in Hell. We can get rid of our bad deeds by asking for Allāh's سبحانه وتعالى forgiveness and doing more good deeds.

Salām

When we meet a Muslim, we say, "*Assalāmu ʿalaykum.*" When we respond, we say, "*Wa ʿalaykumus salām.*"

Cleanliness *(ṭahārah)*: using the toilet

- I go into the toilet with my left foot first and say the *duʿāʾ*.
- I go into the toilet without my socks and use the slippers that are meant to be used in the toilet.
- I should sit down to use the toilet.
- I should not talk in the toilet (unless I need help) and I must not say any *duʿāʾ*.

- When I have finished, I use water and tissue to clean myself.
- Finally, I flush the toilet, wash my hands and leave the toilet with my right foot first and say the *du'ā'*.

Islamic months

The Islamic months are: Muḥarram, Ṣafar, Rabī'ul Awwal, Rabī'uth Thānī, Jumādal Ūlā, Jumādal Ākhirah, Rajab, Sha'bān, Ramaḍān, Shawwāl, Dhul Qa'dah and Dhul Ḥijjah.

Ādāb in the classroom

Practical lesson

Ādāb means good behaviour. We need to show *ādāb* at all times. There are special *ādāb* for when we come to an Islamic school/*madrasah.*

When I come to an Islamic school/*madrasah,* I should:

- Put my shoes, bag and coat away in the right place
- Sit properly where the teacher tells me to sit
- Listen carefully to the teacher
- Put my hands up if I have any questions or want to go to the toilet
- Only answer when the teacher gives permission
- Respect all equipment, especially books
- Respect my classmates and their belongings
- Put away all equipment after using them

- Respect anything with Allāh's سبحانه وتعالى name or our Prophet's صلى الله عليه وسلم name written on it
- Pick up all mess I make before I leave the class

When I come to an Islamic school/*madrasah,* I should make sure that I do not:

- Leave my shoes lying around on the floor
- Leave my bags or belongings lying around
- Run or make noise
- Shout or say bad things
- Make a mess
- Lean on my stool or bench
- Walk over my stool or touch it with my feet
- Eat or drink in class without permission
- Leave my books, worksheets or anything with Arabic on it on the floor
- Disturb other people around me
- Take other people's belongings without asking them
- Argue with or hurt anyone

Bismillāh

Muslims mention the name of Allāh سبحانه وتعالى before they start doing anything. When we say *Bismillāh*, Allāh سبحانه وتعالى rewards us and makes things easy for us.

So, before we do anything we should say:

بِسْمِ اللهِ ***Bismillāh:*** In the name of Allāh

For example, we should say *Bismillāh* before:

- Eating or drinking
- Sleeping
- Before we begin learning
- Wearing clothes
- Leaving our home
- Getting into a car or on a bus or train
- Entering the toilet
- Entering the *masjid*

Allāh سبحانه وتعالى has 99 beautiful names. Two of those names are in *Bismillāhir Raḥmānir Raḥīm*:

- Ar-Raḥmān, which means the Most Merciful.
- Ar-Raḥīm, which means the Most Kind.

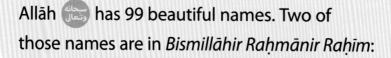

Names of Allāh

Some of the names of Allāh سبحانه وتعالى that we can learn and think about are:

اَلرَّحْمٰنُ	**Ar-Raḥmān**	The Most Merciful
اَلرَّحِيْمُ	**Ar-Raḥīm**	The Most Kind
اَلْعَلِيْمُ	**Al-ʿAlīm**	The All-Knowing
اَلْبَصِيْرُ	**Al-Baṣīr**	The All-Seeing
اَلسَّمِيْعُ	**As-Samīʿ**	The All-Hearing

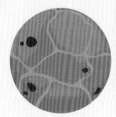

Ar-Raḥmān and Ar-Raḥīm

Allāh سبحانه وتعالى is merciful and kind to everything. Allāh سبحانه وتعالى has given us so many blessings. He has given us perfect eyes, ears, hands, legs and much more. In fact, everything we have is from Allāh سبحانه وتعالى. Therefore, we have to use all of Allāh's سبحانه وتعالى blessings to worship Him and to get close to Him.

The *ḥadīth* of *raḥmah* (mercy)

The Prophet Muḥammad صلى الله عليه وسلم said, "[Allāh] The Most-Kind is kind to people who are kind. Be kind to those on earth, and [Allāh] will be kind to you."[1]

Al-'Alīm, Al-Baṣīr and As-Samī'

Allāh سبحانه وتعالى knows everything. He sees everything and He hears everything. We cannot hide anything from Allāh سبحانه وتعالى.

Imagine a black ant walking on a huge rock on a very, very dark night. Allāh سبحانه وتعالى knows, sees, and hears this ant. Allāh سبحانه وتعالى hears the steps it is taking. He knows where it is going and what the ant is thinking.[2]

[1] Abū Dāwūd, Tirmidhī, Aḥmad; [2] Muslim

Allāh سبحانه وتعالى tells us in the Qur'ān, "Do you not see that Allāh knows everything in the skies and the earth? When three people whisper, Allāh is the fourth with them. When five people whisper, Allāh is the sixth with them; whether it is more [than five] or less [than three], Allāh is with them wherever they are. On the Day of Judgement, He will show them what they have done. Surely, Allāh knows everything." 58:7

Jibrīl teaches us religion

ʿUmar, a Companion of the Prophet says: "One day we were with the Prophet, when a man came to us. He had bright white clothes and dark black hair. None of us knew him and there were no marks on his clothes to show that he had been travelling. The man sat down beside the Prophet. [He] placed his knees against the knees of the Prophet and placed his hands on the Prophet's thighs. He then asked, 'O Muḥammad, tell me about Islām.'

[The Prophet] replied, 'Islām means that you should say there is no god but Allāh and Muḥammad is Allāh's Messenger; and that you should perform *Ṣalāh*, pay *Zakāh* [charity], fast during the month of Ramaḍān, and do *Ḥaj* if you can go there.'

[The man] said, 'You have spoken the truth.' We were surprised that the man asked questions and then said, 'You have spoken the truth.'

He then said, 'Now tell me about *īmān*.' The Prophet ﷺ replied, 'It means that you should believe in Allāh, His angels, His books, His messengers, the Last Day, and that you should believe in destiny, both the good and the bad.' The man again said, 'You have spoken the truth.'

Then he asked, 'Now, tell me about *iḥsān*.' The Prophet ﷺ replied, 'It means that you should worship Allāh as if you see Him, but if you cannot do this then you should know that He sees you.'

He then asked, 'Now tell me about the Hour [Day of Judgement]'. The Prophet ﷺ replied, 'The one being asked about it does not know more than the one who is asking.' [In other words, the Prophet ﷺ said that he did not know when the the Day of Judgement will happen].

So the man said, 'then tell me about its signs.' The Prophet ﷺ replied, '....You will see shepherds so poor [they will have] no shoes or clothes, competing with each other to see who can build the tallest buildings.'"

‘Umar رضي الله عنه says, “[The man] went away and I stayed behind for a while. The Prophet صلى الله عليه وسلم said to me, ‘Do you know who that man was, O ‘Umar?’ I replied, ‘Allāh and His Messenger know best.’ The Prophet صلى الله عليه وسلم said, ‘He was Jibrīl, who came to teach you your religion.’”[1]

Lessons

There are five pillars in Islām and Muslims must follow them. They are:

1. ***Shahādah*** - saying that there is no god but Allāh سبحانه وتعالى and that Muḥammad صلى الله عليه وسلم is Allāh’s Messenger).
2. ***Ṣalāh*** - Five daily prayers.

[1] Muslim

Shepherds will compete in building tall buildings.

3. Ṣawm - Fasting.

4. Zakāh - charity; money that rich Muslims give to the poor.

5. Ḥajj - Pilgrimage.

The *ḥadīth* also tells teaches us six beliefs Muslims must have:

1. Belief in Allāh سبحانه وتعالى.
2. Belief in His angels.
3. Belief in Allāh's سبحانه وتعالى Books.
4. Belief in Allāh's سبحانه وتعالى Messengers.
5. Belief in the Last Day (Day of Judgement).
6. Belief in *qadar* (destiny or fate).

Five pillars of Islām

There are five pillars in Islām, which every Muslim must act upon. These are:

1. Shahādah (to bear witness)

To say and believe in:

اَشْهَدُ اَنْ لَّآ اِلٰهَ اِلَّا اللّٰهُ وَاَشْهَدُ اَنَّ مُحَمَّدًا عَبْدُهٗ وَرَسُوْلُهٗ

"Ash hadu al-lā ilāha illallāhu wa ash hadu anna Muḥammadan 'abduhū wa rasūluh."

This means, "I bear witness that there is no god but Allāh and I bear witness that Muḥammad is His servant and messenger."

All Muslims believe in one God and that Muḥammad ﷺ is the last and final Messenger. There will be no other messengers after him.

2. *Ṣalāh* (prayer)

Muslims must perform *Ṣalāh* five times a day, every day. The names of these prayers are: *Fajr*, *Ẓuhr*, *'Asr*, *Maghrib* and *'Ishā'*.

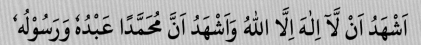

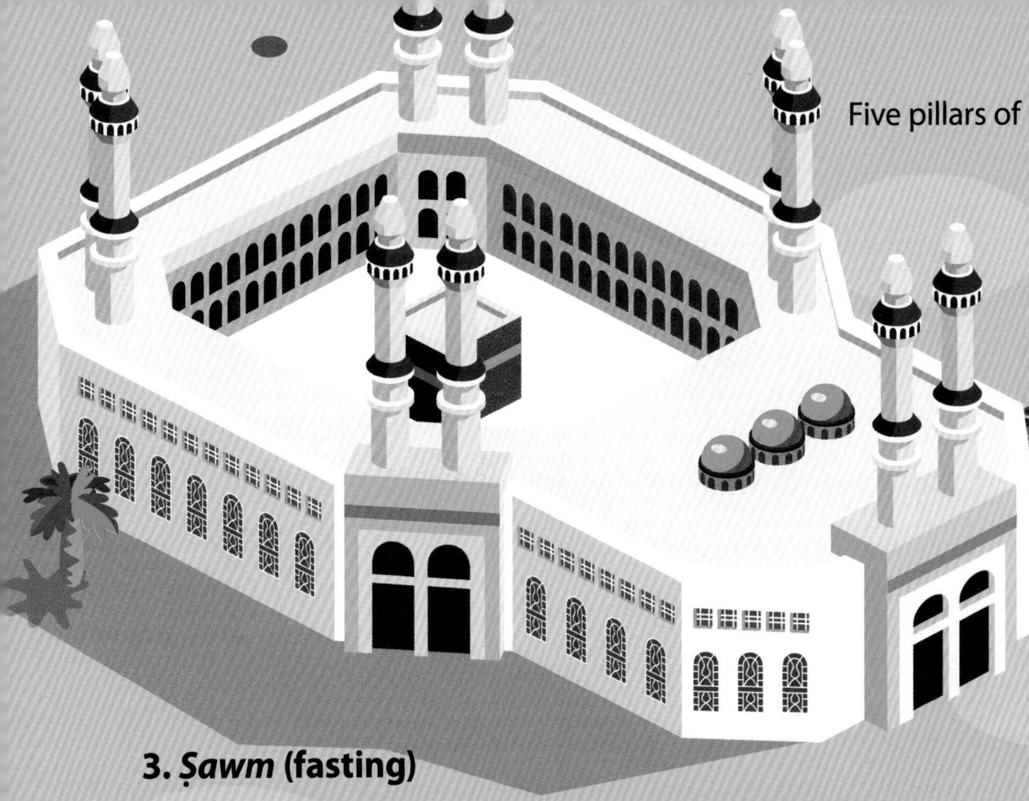

3. *Ṣawm* (fasting)

Muslims should fast in the month of Ramaḍān. This is called *Ṣawm* in Arabic. Fasting means not to eat or drink from the beginning of *Fajr* until *Maghrib*, every day during Ramaḍān.

4. *Zakāh* (charity)

A rich Muslim must give *Zakāh*. *Zakāh* is a small amount of money that a rich Muslim gives to poor people each year

5. *Ḥajj* (pilgrimage)

Muslims must go to the Kaʿbah in Makkah and perform *Ḥajj* at least once in their life if they can afford it.

Before Prophet Ādam

A long, long time ago after Allāh سبحانه وتعالى made the world, He decorated it with mountains, oceans and trees. Some parts of the world were hot and dry, while other parts were cool and wet. After some time, Allāh سبحانه وتعالى created jinns and sent them to earth.

Jinns

Allāh سبحانه وتعالى created jinns from a smokeless fire. He gave them all different powers: some can fly, and some can change their shape; others are strong, and they can build amazing things.

Allāh سبحانه وتعالى created jinns for His worship, and like human beings, they have the choice to do good or bad. If they worship Allāh سبحانه وتعالى and do good deeds, they will go to Paradise. However, if they disobey Allāh سبحانه وتعالى and do bad deeds, they will be punished in Hell.

As time went by, many jinns began to act wickedly. However, there was one jinn who was really good and obedient to Allāh سبحانه وتعالى. Because of this, he was given permission to live in the heavens with the angels. This jinn was very clever and worshipped Allāh سبحانه وتعالى a lot. He worshipped so much that soon, Allāh سبحانه وتعالى allowed him to be with some of the great and important angels.

A new creation

One day, Allāh سبحانه وتعالى spoke to all the angels and this jinn, and He told them about a new creation. They were all surprised. The angels thought that because jinns had behaved badly before on earth, the new creation would also behave badly. They asked: "Are you going
2 30 to create on earth those who will do bad things and kill one another, while we sing your praises?"

"Surely, I know things you do not," replied Allāh سبحانه وتعالى. This new creation was the first human being; he was Prophet Ādam عليه السلام.

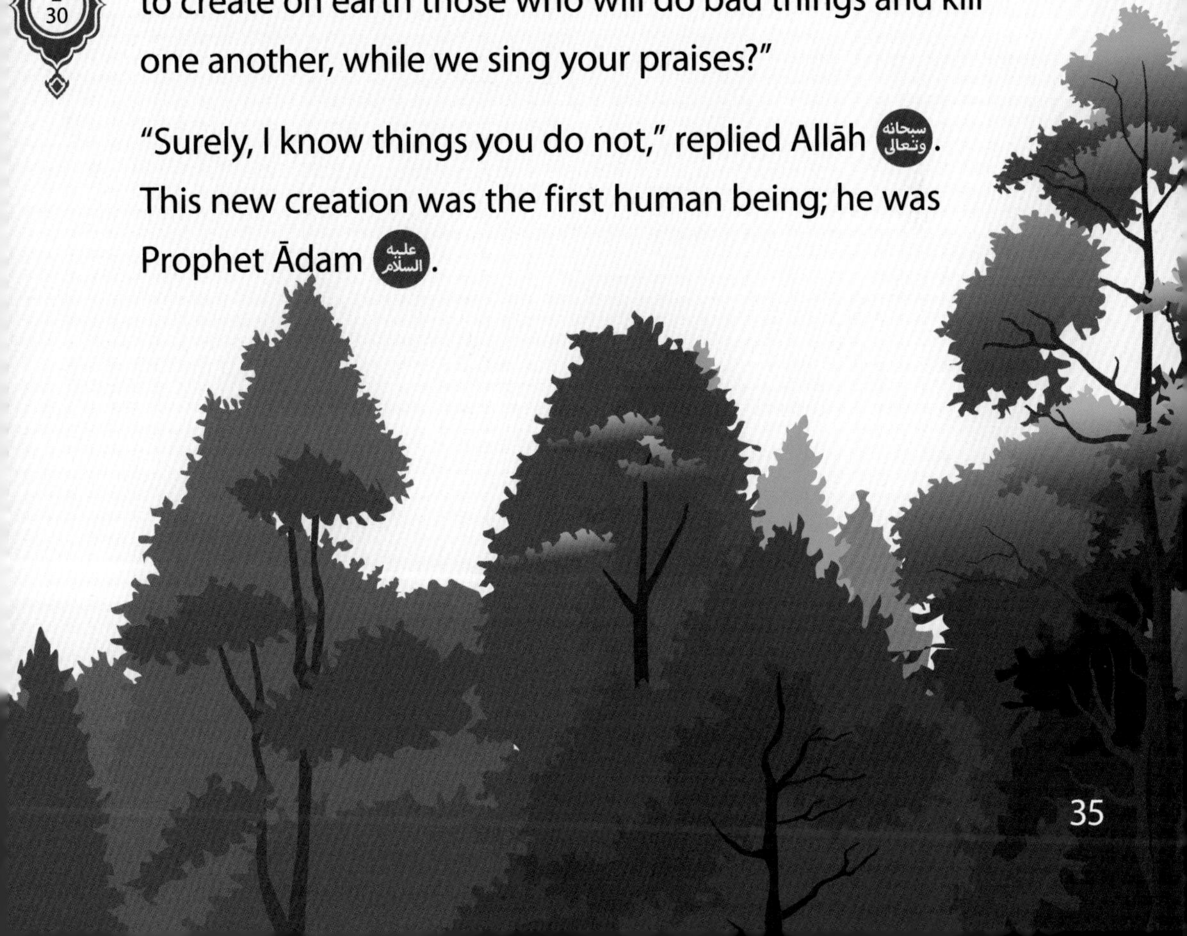

Six articles of faith

There are six basic things a Muslim must believe in. They are called the six articles of faith.

1. Belief in one God

Muslims believe that there is only one God, Allāh ﷾. He has created everything. There have never been any other gods at all, and there will never be any other god besides Him.

Allāh ﷾ is Merciful and Kind. He has no mother, father or children. Muslims believe in Allāh ﷾ and obey His commands so that they can enter Jannah.

There are six basic things a Muslim must believe in.

2. Belief in angels

Muslims believe in angels. Allāh ﷾ created the angels from light. They do not eat, sleep or drink and they always obey and worship Allāh ﷾. Only Allāh ﷾ knows the total number of angels. Each angel has a duty; some angels write down all the good and bad things we do.

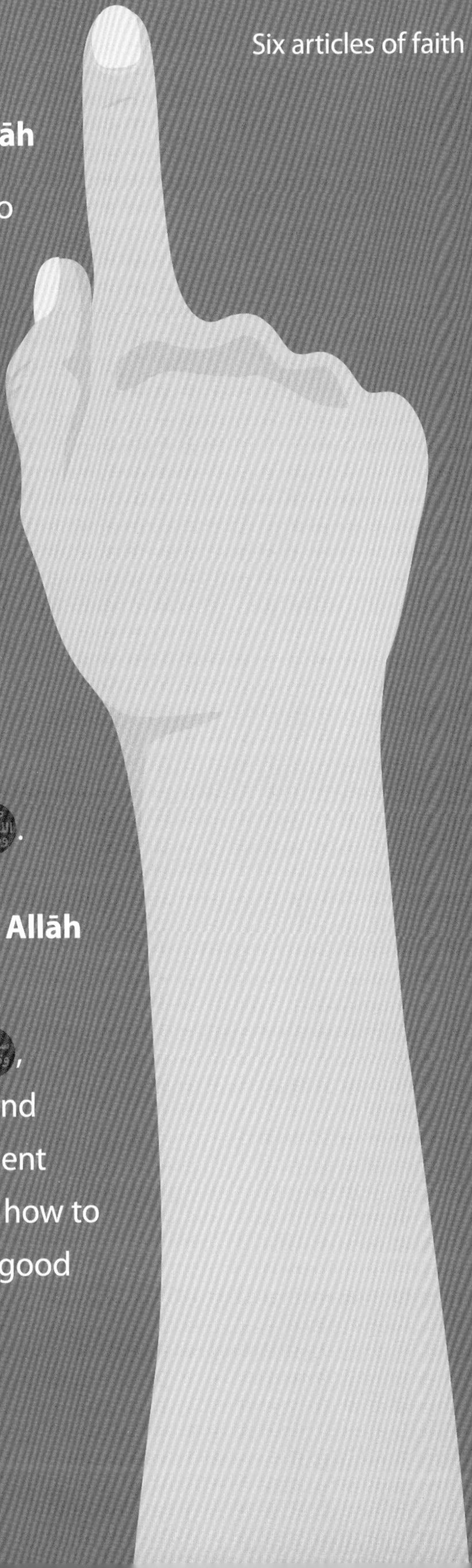

3. Belief in the books of Allāh

Allāh سبحانه وتعالى sent many books to His messengers, including:

1. The Tawrāh (Torah), revealed to Prophet Mūsā عليه السلام.
2. The Zabūr (Psalms), revealed to Prophet Dāwūd عليه السلام.
3. The Injīl, revealed to Prophet ʿĪsā عليه السلام.
4. The Qurʾān, revealed to Prophet Muḥammad صلى الله عليه وسلم.

4. Belief in the prophets of Allāh

Muslims believe in all the messengers sent by Allāh سبحانه وتعالى, such as Nūḥ, Mūsā, ʿĪsā عليهم السلام and Muḥammad صلى الله عليه وسلم. Allāh سبحانه وتعالى sent messengers to teach people how to worship Him and how to be good people.

5. Belief in life after death and the Day of Judgement

Muslims believe that one day, the world will come to an end. Everyone who has passed away will be brought back to life on the Day of Judgement.

The angels write down in books, all the good and bad actions that people do. Allāh سبحانه وتعالى will take out these books and weigh them on the Day of Judgement. If people were good in the world and obeyed His commands, they will enter Jannah (Paradise). If they were bad and disobeyed His commands, they will enter Jahannam (Hell), unless He forgives them.

6. Belief in destiny (*qadar*)

Muslims believe in destiny, which is called *qadar* in Arabic. This means that all good and bad is from Allāh سبحانه وتعالى. He has written everything that will happen, both good and bad, but people still make their own choices when they do good or bad deeds.

Ādam's creation

Ādam عليه السلام was the first human to be created. Allāh created Ādam عليه السلام from clay. Then Allāh سبحانه وتعالى taught Ādam عليه السلام the names of all things, making him a very special creation.

Allāh سبحانه وتعالى commanded all the angels and the jinn who stayed with them to prostrate (make a *sajdah*) to Ādam عليه السلام, out of respect. They all obeyed Allāh سبحانه وتعالى except for this jinn who refused to do so.

Allāh سبحانه وتعالى asked him, "What stopped you from prostrating when I commanded you?" He replied, "I am better than him! You have created him from clay and me out of fire". So Allāh سبحانه وتعالى said to him, "Get out of here! You are cursed and the curse will be on you until the Day of Judgement". This jinn asked Allāh سبحانه وتعالى if he could live till the Day of Judgment. After Allāh سبحانه وتعالى gave him permission, the jinn said, "Because You have thrown me out, I will try and lead people away from You and make them disobey You, except for Your good servants." Allāh سبحانه وتعالى replied, "I will fill up Hell with you and those who follow you!"

This jinn lost all hope in Allāh's سبحانه وتعالى mercy so his name became Iblīs, 'the one who lost all hope in Allāh سبحانه وتعالى. Iblīs' jealousy and hate for Ādam عليه السلام made him become ungrateful of his own blessings. This ungratefulness and hatred of Ādam led him to become the hateful Satan (Shayṭān).

Meanwhile, Ādam عليه السلام lived in Paradise and enjoyed all its wonders. However, Ādam عليه السلام felt lonely on his own. So one day, while he sat with his eyes closed thinking about his loneliness, Allāh سبحانه وتعالى created Ḥawwā' رضي الله عنها. After opening his eyes, Ādam عليه السلام was pleased to see someone that would give him company.

Both of them were allowed to stay in Paradise and eat whatever they wanted. However, they were warned not to eat from one particular tree.

Some time passed and Iblīs came to them both and
whispered evil thoughts. He said, "Shall I tell you
of the everlasting tree? If you eat from its fruits you 7 20
will become two angels or live forever." He swore by
Allāh سبحانه وتعالى that he was telling the truth. Up till then,
Ādam عليه السلام had never heard anyone taking Allāh's سبحانه وتعالى
name and lying. So, he believed Iblīs and was tricked
into eating the forbidden fruit.

Deeds

Why have we been sent to this world?

We have been sent to this world to do good actions (deeds). Those who do good deeds will be rewarded with Paradise (Jannah). Those who do bad deeds may be punished in Hell (Jahannam) unless Allāh سبحانه وتعالى forgives them.

Good deeds

Everything good we do is written in our Book of Good Deeds. For every good deed, Allāh سبحانه وتعالى will give us ten rewards or more. Our rewards will lead us to Jannah.

Good deeds we can do:

- Be kind to one another
- Respect our parents
- Share our favourite things
- Pray and study well
- Give in charity

Can you think of more good deeds we can do to earn lots of reward?

Bad deeds

All bad things we do are written down in our Book of Bad Deeds. For every bad deed we do, we get a sin. Sins can lead to Jahannam. We need to avoid bad deeds such as:

- Lying
- Swearing
- Fighting
- Stealing
- Bullying or being mean to people

Can you think of more bad deeds we need to avoid?

Our good and bad deeds will be weighed on the Day of Judgement. If our good deeds are more, Allāh سبحانه وتعالى will reward us with Paradise. If our bad deeds are more, we may be in trouble.

We can get rid of our bad deeds by saying sorry to people and asking Allāh سبحانه وتعالى to forgive us.

Jannah

People who do good and listen to Allāh سبحانه وتعالى will go to Jannah (Paradise). Jannah is a very beautiful place. It will have palaces made of gold and silver. It will also have amazing rivers of milk and honey. It will be full of treasure and have mountains of tasty food.

Every time you eat, the food will taste better and better. In fact, every bite and every sip will be better than the one before. You can have whatever you want in Jannah, such as rivers of chocolate, cars that fly, palaces made from sweets and much more!

No matter how many sweets you have, you will not get a toothache or a stomach ache. There will be no problems or pain in Jannah. You will never grow old or get bored. You will also live with your friends and family and have fun every day. Everyone will love to go to Jannah.

Jahannam

On the Day of Judgement, Allāh سبحانه وتعالى will punish those who disobeyed Him. His greatest punishment will be to put someone into Jahannam (Hell).

Jahannam is a scary place. No one will want to go there. Prophet Muḥammad صلى الله عليه وسلم has told us to save ourselves from Jahannam by doing good deeds, even if it is by giving something small in charity, or by saying a good word.[1]

We always need to think about what we do and say, and how we behave with others. We also need to do lots of good deeds to keep away from Jahannam. If we do anything bad, we should ask Allāh سبحانه وتعالى to forgive us. Prophet Muḥammad صلى الله عليه وسلم taught us to ask Allāh سبحانه وتعالى again and again, to save us from the fire of Jahannam.

[1] Bukhārī and Muslim.

Ādam on Earth

When Ādam and Ḥawwā' عليهم السلام ate from the forbidden tree, their clothes suddenly vanished! They both began to cover themselves with leaves.

Allāh سبحانه وتعالى said to them, "Did I not forbid you from that tree and say to you that Satan was an open enemy to you?" Ādam and Ḥawwā' عليهم السلام realised their mistake. They asked Allāh سبحانه وتعالى for forgiveness saying, "Our Lord!
7 23 We have done wrong to ourselves; if you do not forgive us and have mercy on us, we will surely be from the losers."

Allāh سبحانه وتعالى answered their prayer and forgave them. However, they were not allowed to stay in Paradise. Instead, they were told to live on earth for the rest of their lives. Iblīs was also sent to earth. Allāh سبحانه وتعالى warned Ādam and Ḥawwā' عليهم السلام about Iblīs and his tricks.

On earth, Ādam and Ḥawwā' عليهم السلام had many children. Amongst their children were Hābīl and Qābīl.

One day, Hābīl and Qābīl offered some charity to Allāh سبحانه وتعالى and left this on a hill. In those days, if a whirlwind of fire came and took the charity, it meant that Allāh سبحانه وتعالى had accepted it.

A whirlwind came but only Hābīl's charity was taken up. Qābīl became very jealous and out of anger, wanted to kill Hābīl. Hābīl tried to tell his brother that it was wrong, but Qābīl did not listen and killed his brother.

Afterwards, Qābīl felt really guilty and sad. At first, he did not know what to do with the body of his brother, but later, managed to bury him.

Manners and friends

There are four *aḥādīth* that teach us the rules to follow and good manners to have with everyone around us:

1. "Whoever believes in Allāh سبحانه وتعالى and the Last Day, let them speak what is good or keep quiet…"[1]
2. "From the excellence of a person's Islām, is to leave alone those things which do not concern them."[2]
3. "Do not become angry."[3]
4. "None of you have true belief until they love for their brother/sister what they love for themselves."[4]

We learn from these *aḥādīth* that:

- We should only speak when we have something good to say.
- We should never use bad language or hurt others.
- We should control our anger.
- We should always share the things we love.
- We should wish the best for everyone.
- We should respect our parents and elders.

Remember the golden rule of good manners: "Treat people the way you like to be treated by others."

 [1,3,4,5] Bukhārī, [2] Tirmidhī

Prophet Muḥammad صلى الله عليه وسلم said: "A good friend is like a person carrying musk and a bad friend is like a blacksmith. The one who is carrying musk will either give you some perfume as a present; you will buy some from him; or you will at least find a lovely smell just by staying with him. However, the one who is a blacksmith will either burn your clothes or just by staying with him, you will find a nasty smell."[5]

We learn the following from the *ḥadīth*:

- We should choose good people as our friends.
- Good friends will have a good affect on us.
- We should stay away from bad people.
- Bad friends will have a bad affect on us.

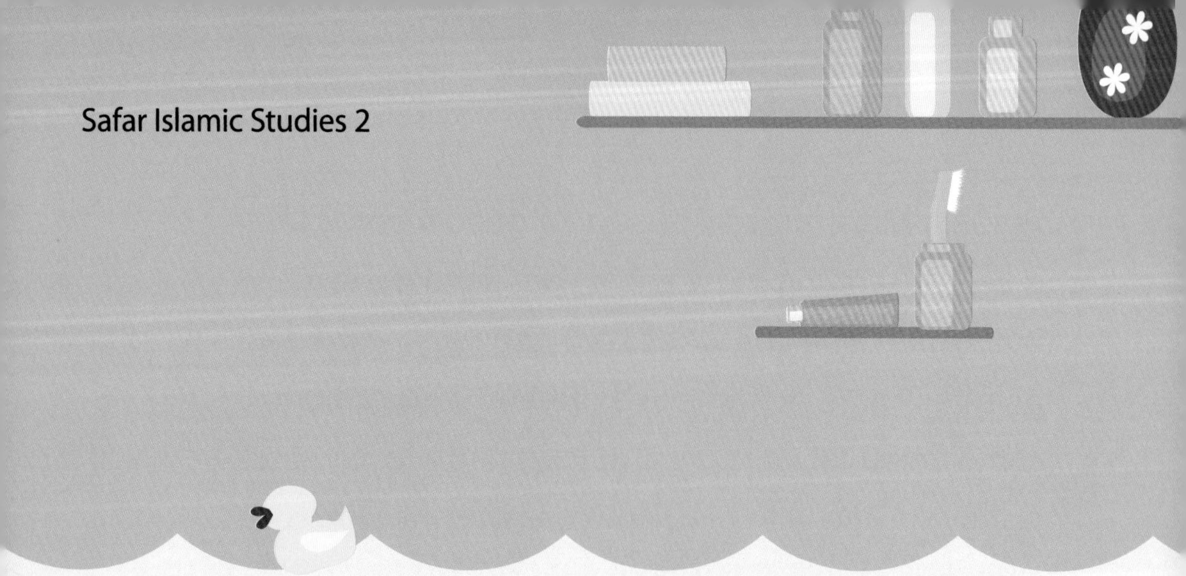

Basic cleanliness

The Prophet ﷺ said, "Keeping clean is half of faith."[1] Keeping clean is very important in Islām. Muslims should always be clean and wear clean clothes. Keeping clean is called *ṭahārah* in Arabic. *Ṭahārah* does not only mean wearing clean clothes or having a clean body. It also means doing *wuḍū'* and *ghusl*.

Ghusl

Ghusl means to clean the entire body by taking a bath or a shower. During *ghusl*, we should make sure we wash all our body and hair and rinse our mouth and nose properly.

[1] Muslim

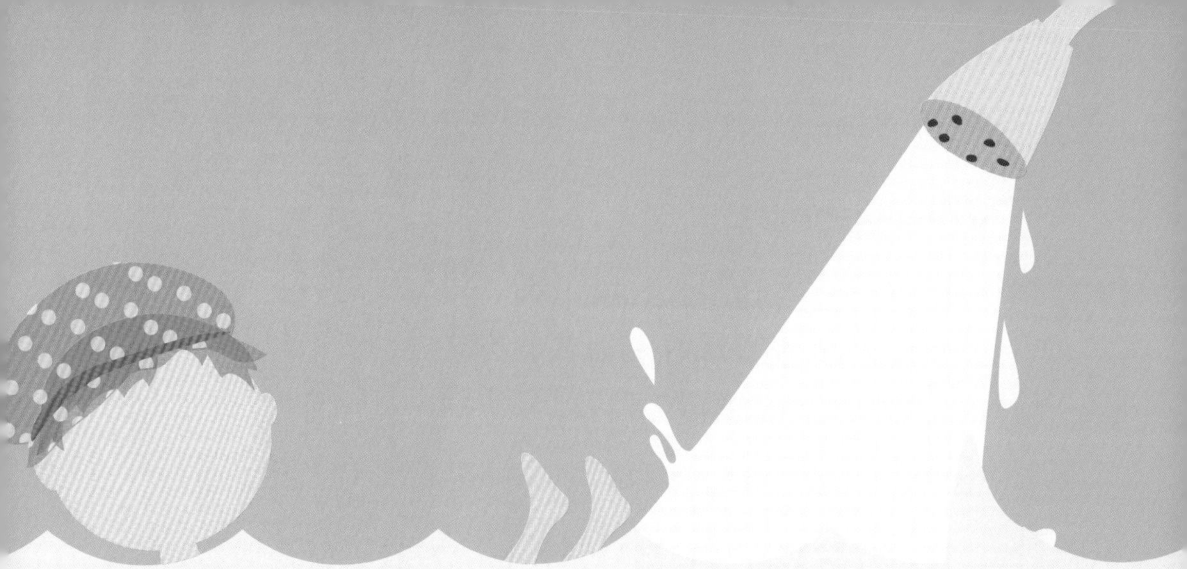

The Prophet ﷺ used to have a bath regularly. He also had a bath on Fridays before the *Jumu'ah* prayer. We should follow the way of the Prophet ﷺ by having baths regularly, especially on Fridays.

Wuḍū'

Wuḍū' means to wash some parts of the body using water. We must make sure our bodies and clothes are clean before we perform *wuḍū*. We need to perform *wuḍū* before *Ṣalāh* or before touching the Qur'ān.

The Prophet ﷺ said, "The key to Paradise is prayer and the key to prayer is *wuḍū'*."[2] *Ṣalāh* will not be accepted without *wuḍū'* and Allāh سبحانه وتعالى will not let people into Paradise without *Ṣalāh*.

[2] Tirmidhī

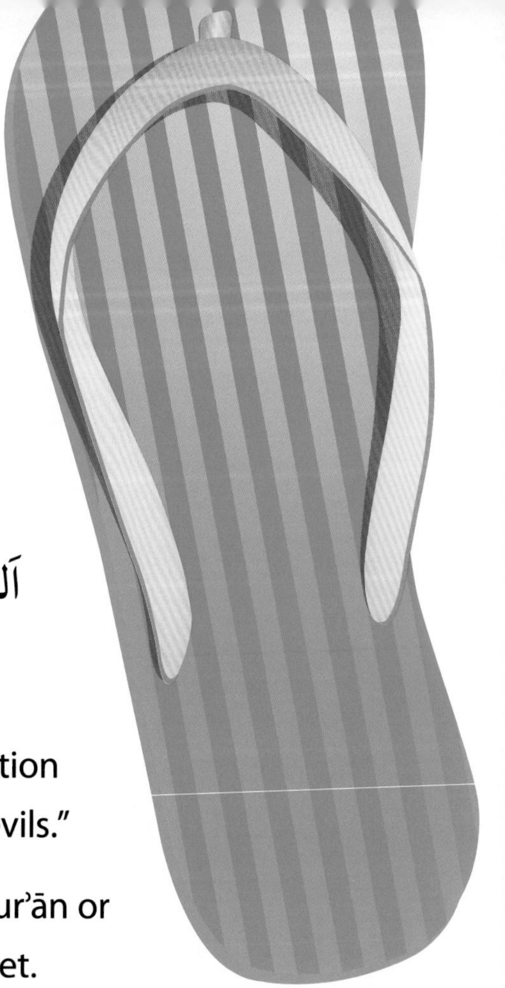

Using the toilet

We should go into the toilet with our left foot first, and say this *du'ā'* before entering the toilet:

اَللّٰهُمَّ إِنِّـيْ أَعُوْذُ بِكَ مِنَ الْخُبُثِ وَالْخَبَائِثِ

"O Allāh, I ask for your protection from the male and female devils."

We should not talk, read the Qur'ān or say Allāh's (سبحانه وتعالى) name in the toilet.

We should not go into the toilet barefoot because the floor may be dirty. We should take off our socks before going to the toilet to make sure the socks do not become wet or unclean.

We should wipe the toilet seat to make sure it is clean before we sit down. We should always sit and use the toilet; standing up and using the toilet makes the toilet seat and clothes unclean, and this can lead to Allāh's (سبحانه وتعالى) punishment in the grave.

Cleaning ourselves

When we have finished, we should wash ourselves to become clean. First, wipe the unclean area with tissue using the left hand. Then, holding a jug of water with the right hand, wash the unclean area using the left hand. This is called *istinjāʾ* in Arabic.

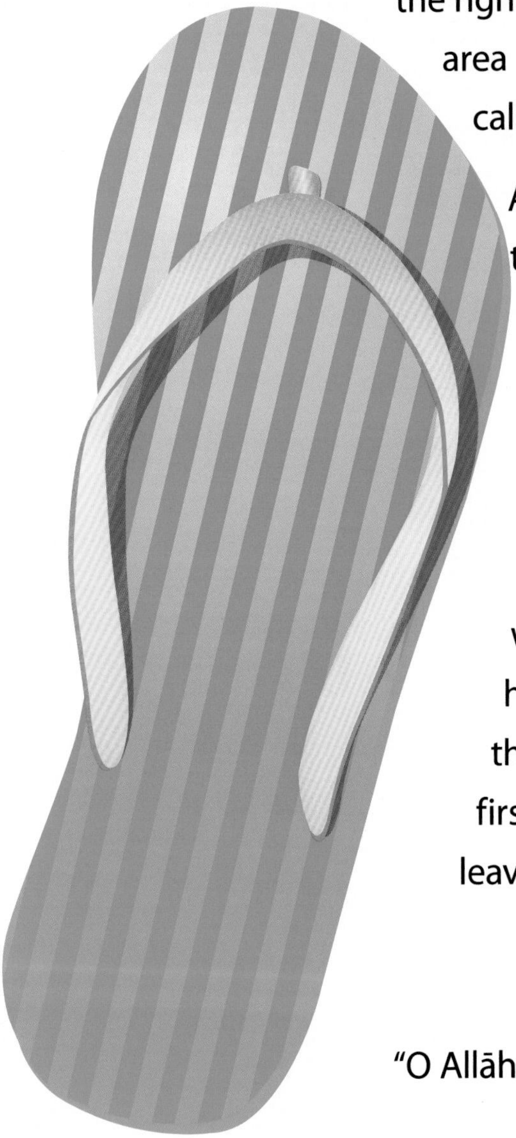

After you finish, wipe the toilet seat with tissue to make sure it is clean and then flush the toilet. This will leave it clean for the next person to use.

We must remember to wash our hands when we have finished. Then, leave the toilet with the right foot first. Finally, say the *duʿāʾ* when leaving the toilet:

غُفْرَانَكَ

"O Allāh, I ask for your forgiveness."

When and how to perform wuḍūʾ

We must perform *wuḍūʾ* whenever we want to:

- Perform *Ṣalāh,*
- Touch the Qurʾān.

We should also make a habit of doing *wuḍūʾ*:

- Before we go to sleep,
- After waking up,
- Before going outside,
- Before going to the *masjid,*
- Before learning and touching books of knowledge.

Peforming *wuḍū'*

Practical lesson

1. Make intention to perform *wuḍū'* and say *Bismillāh*.
2. Wash the right hand including the wrist three times, and then wash the left hand including the wrists three times.
3. Rinse the mouth three times.
4. Rinse the nose three times.
5. Wash the face three times.
6. Wash the right arm including the elbow three times, and then wash the left arm including the elbow three times.
7. Wipe the head once.
8. Wipe the ears and the back of the neck once.
9. Wash the right foot including the ankle three times, and then wash the left foot including the ankle, three times.

Prophet Nūḥ

Allāh سبحانه وتعالى blessed Ādam عليه السلام with many children and grandchildren, so the number of people in the world increased very quickly. People built many towns and lived happily, worshipping Allāh سبحانه وتعالى alone.

Since Shayṭān was thrown out of Paradise, he knew that he would go to Hell. He also knew that the children of Ādam عليه السلام who worshipped Allāh سبحانه وتعالى would go to Paradise. This made Shayṭān very angry. He was full of hate and jealousy, and began to plan on how he could take all the children of Ādam عليه السلام to Hell with him.

Shayṭān's evil plan

Shayṭān knew that the worst sin anyone can do is to worship someone or something other than Allāh سبحانه وتعالى. This is called *shirk*. He also knew that Allāh سبحانه وتعالى forgives all sins except *shirk*. "This would certainly be the best way to take people to Hell," he thought.

Shayṭān knew that he could not openly ask people to worship statues. People knew it is wrong and they would say, "How can we worship other things with Allāh when He is our only creator!?"

So, Shayṭān made an evil plan to slowly make people do *shirk*. He knew that people loved and showed great respect to men who were very close to Allāh سبحانه وتعالى. Shayṭān asked people about the religious men that had passed away and how much they missed them. He told them, "Why don't you look at them everyday to remember them?" The people asked, "How can we do that when they are dead?" He told them, "Draw pictures of these men and look at them every morning."

So, people drew pictures of religious men to help remember them. Shayṭān slowly made people change the pictures into statues. The people now had statues in their homes and places of worship. They still worshipped Allāh سبحانه وتعالى alone, but used the statues to remember the dead and to show respect to them.

As time passed, younger generations saw their parents showing great respect to the statues and praying to Allāh سبحانه وتعالى near them. When their parents passed away, the children copied them without understanding the reason why the statues were made. They then, slowly, began to directly pray to the statues and worship them. They also began sacrificing animals for them. People had been tricked by Shayṭān's evil plan. They were now worshipping statues instead of Allāh سبحانه وتعالى.

Prophet Nūḥ عليه السلام

Allāh سبحانه وتعالى became upset with such people. He had created them, gave them food, water, clothes, shelter and so much more. Yet, they did not worship Him. So Allāh سبحانه وتعالى took away some blessings but people still did not turn back to Him or ask Him for forgiveness.

However, there was one man who was different. He was pious and truthful, and a man who had never worshipped statues. His name was Nūḥ عليه السلام. So, Allāh سبحانه وتعالى sent him to his people to teach them the right way to worship Allāh سبحانه وتعالى.

Actions that break wuḍūʾ

The following are common actions that break a person's *wuḍū*ʾ:

1. Sleeping
2. Using the toilet
3. Passing wind
4. Bleeding
5. Laughing loudly in *Ṣalāh*
6. Vomiting

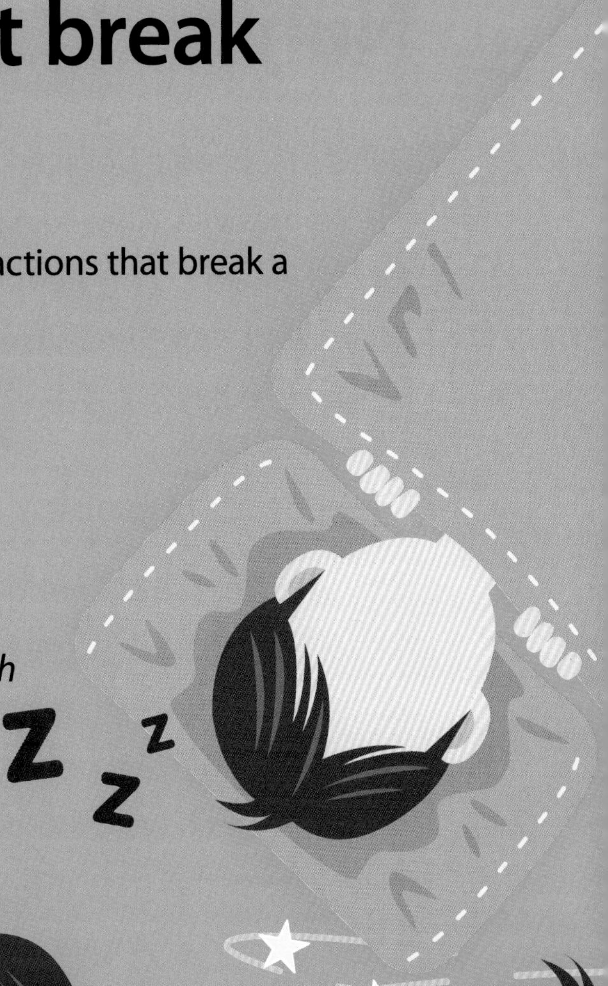

Nūḥ builds the ark

Nūḥ's عليه السلام people believed that worshipping idols
and statues was allowed. So Nūḥ عليه السلام began to advise
them. He said: "O my people! Worship Allāh, you have
7 59 no god but Him. Surely, I fear for you the punishment
of a terrible day."

The people's response

However, people did not believe Nūḥ عليه السلام and accused him of lying. Nūḥ عليه السلام tried very hard and spent many years advising people to stop worshipping idols. However, only a few poor and weak people listened to him. The rich were too proud to listen and thought they were better than everyone else. They used to say to Nūḥ عليه السلام, "We are great people and those who follow you are poor! Why should we believe you when only the weak follow you!?"

The patience of Nuḥ عليه السلام

Nūḥ عليه السلام continued calling people to Allāh سبحانه وتعالى but they never listened. Some would even put their fingers in their ears when he spoke to them. However,

Nūḥ (عليه السلام) remained strong and continued calling them to Allāh (سبحانه وتعالى). Nūḥ (عليه السلام) also told his people that if they did not obey Allāh (سبحانه وتعالى), they would soon be punished.

11:32 Like this, 950 years went by, and then his people began to say, "Nūḥ! You have argued with us, and you have argued many times, so bring us what you promised if you are telling the truth!".

Nūḥ عليه السلام knew that no one else would accept his message. Allāh سبحانه وتعالى already told Nūḥ عليه السلام, "None of your people will believe except those who have already believed." For this reason, Nūḥ عليه السلام made *duʿāʾ*. He said, "O Allāh, do not leave a single disbeliever on earth!"

The ark

Allāh سبحانه وتعالى answered Nūḥ's *duʿāʾ* and ordered him to build an ark. Nūḥ عليه السلام began building the ark far away from the sea in a hot, dry place. When people saw him building the ark, they began to laugh and make fun of him. "Where is this ship going to go, Nūḥ? Is it going to sail on land or climb up the mountains!" they joked and laughed.

People began to laugh and make fun of Nūḥ and the ark.

Nūḥ عليه السلام heard them laugh and make fun of him but he was always patient and did not give up. He knew that the promise of Allāh سبحانه وتعالى will come true.

How to perform ghusl

Ghusl means to have a bath or a shower. We should perform *ghusl* as often as possible, especially when we become dirty. The Prophet ﷺ used to have a bath regularly, especially before the *Jumuʿah* (Friday) prayer.

How to perform *ghusl*

Practical lesson

1. Start by washing both hands.
2. Perform *wuḍūʾ*.
3. Wash your mouth by gargling.
4. Rinse the nose.
5. Pour water over your hair and the whole body.

Nūḥ and the flood

Nūḥ عليه السلام called his people to Allāh سبحانه وتعالى for over 950 years. He tried his best and stayed patient. Now it was time for them to see Allāh's سبحانه وتعالى promise come true.

The storm

A huge storm appeared and it began to rain heavily. Soon, there was water everywhere. Allāh سبحانه وتعالى ordered Nūḥ عليه السلام to take his family, all the believers and two of every animal on to the ark. The flood would be so great that no human or animal would stay alive.

As the water kept rising, people climbed on every hilltop and mountain to escape the punishment. They were warned but did not believe. Now, the people who made fun of Nūḥ عليه السلام had nowhere to go.

Nūḥ عليه السلام had a son who was also a disbeliever. When Nūḥ عليه السلام saw his son in the flood, he said to him,

"My son! Come on board and do not be with the disbelievers." His son replied, "I will go to the mountain 11 42
and it will protect me from the water". So Nūḥ عليه السلام said to him, "Today, nothing will protect you from Allāh's سبحانه وتعالى command." Then the waves came between them and Nūḥ's عليه السلام son drowned.

After the flood

After the people were punished, the rain stopped and the water went away. The ark stopped on Mount Jūdiy, and Allāh سبحانه وتعالى said, "Nūḥ, come down in peace".

Allāh سبحانه وتعالى saved Nūḥ عليه السلام, the believers and all the animals. They all lived in peace and the world was filled with the children of Nūḥ عليه السلام and the believers.

Lessons

- We should be patient and strong and not give up.
- We should always have hope in Allāh سبحانه وتعالى.
- If a lot of people do something wrong, it still does not make it right.
- Only Allāh سبحانه وتعالى guides people to the straight path
- Allāh سبحانه وتعالى does not look at people's family but He looks at what they do.

The boy and the king

Long ago, there lived a king who had a magician. When the magician became old, he said to the king, "I am old and my time is nearly over. Send me a boy whom I can teach magic." So, the king sent him a boy.

Whenever the boy went to the magician, he passed by a monk along the way. One day, the boy decided to sit with the monk and listen to his words. He began to like the monk. However, he would get late and the magician would get angry at him. So, the boy complained about this to the monk. The monk said to him, "Whenever you are afraid of the magician, say to him, 'My family kept me busy.' And whenever you are afraid of your family, say to them, 'The magician kept me busy.' Thus, the boy carried on like this for some time without getting in trouble.

The test

One day, a huge creature appeared on the road and people were unable to pass. The boy said, "Today, I shall know whether the magician is better or the monk." He then took a stone and said, "O Allāh! If what the monk does is better than what the magician does, kill this creature so people can cross." He then hit the creature with the stone and killed it.

The boy came to the monk and told him about what happened. The monk said to him, "O my son! Today you are better than me, but you may be arrested. If you are arrested, do not tell them about me."

The blind man

The boy could now cure the blind and the sick. A close friend of the king who had lost his eyesight heard about this special boy and visited him bringing many gifts. He said, "Cure me and you shall have these gifts." "I do not cure anybody, replied the boy. "It is only Allāh who cures people. So, believe in Allāh and ask Him; He will cure you." The man believed in Allāh سبحانه وتعالى and prayed to Him, and Allāh سبحانه وتعالى cured him.

When the man visited the king, the king asked, "Who gave you back your sight?" The man replied, "My Lord." The king asked, "Me?" The man said, "No, my Lord and your Lord, Allāh." The king asked angrily, "Do you have another Lord beside me?" The man replied, "Yes, your Lord and my Lord is Allāh سبحانه وتعالى."

The king became very angry and hurt the man until he found out about the boy. So, the boy was brought to the king who asked: "O boy! Has your magic become so powerful that you can cure the blind, the sick and those with other diseases?" The boy said, "I do not cure anyone. Only the Lord can cure." The king asked, "Me?" The boy replied, "No!" The king yelled, "Do you have another Lord besides me!" The boy answered, "My Lord and your Lord is Allāh." So, the king hurt the boy until he learnt about the monk.

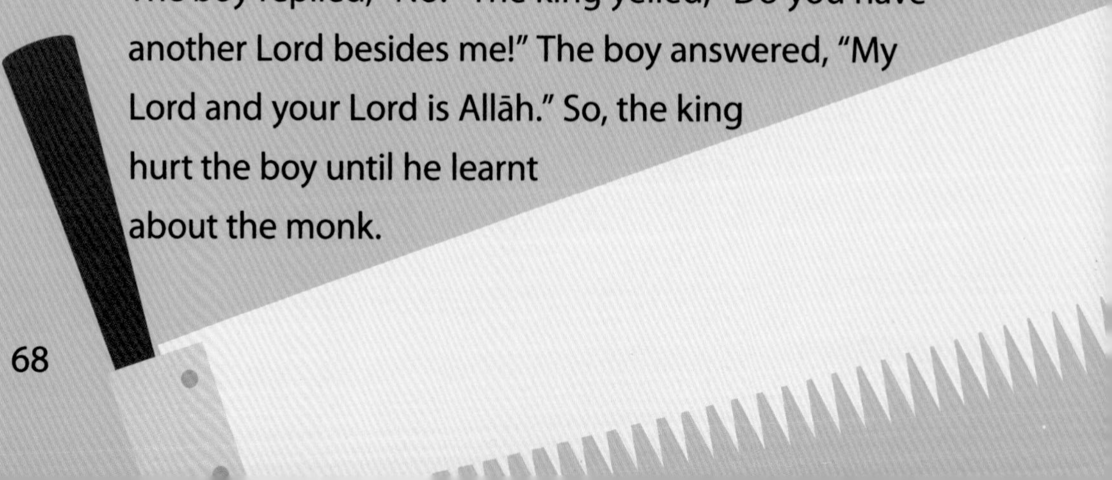

Then, the monk was brought to the king and was ordered to leave his religion. The monk refused, so the king killed the monk. Then it was said to the man who used to be blind, "Leave your religion." But he too refused, and he was also killed.

The brave boy

The boy was also brought and ordered to leave his religion, but he refused. So, the king ordered his guards to take the boy to the top of a mountain and see if the boy leaves his religion. If he refuses, he told the guards to throw the boy off the mountain. The guards took the boy and when they reached the top, the boy said, "O Allāh! Save me from them however You wish." So, the mountain shook and they all fell down. The boy came back to the king and the king asked, "Where are the guards?" The boy said, "Allāh saved me from them."

The king then ordered more guards to take the boy to the middle of the sea. He said to them, "If he leaves his religion, let him go but if he refuses, throw him into the sea!" So, they took him to the sea. The boy again said, "O Allāh! Save me from them however You wish." All of the guards drowned except the boy.

The pits of fire

The boy returned to the king and the king again asked, "Where are the guards?" The boy replied, "Allāh saved me from them." Then he said to the king, "You will not be able to hurt me until you do as I order you."

The king asked, "What should I do?" The boy said, "Gather the people in a high place and tie me to the trunk of a tree. Then take an arrow and say, 'In the name of Allāh, the Lord of the boy.' If you do this, you will be able to hurt me."

So, the king placed an arrow in a bow and shot it, saying, "In the name of Allāh, the Lord of the boy." The arrow hit the boy and he died. Seeing this, the people shouted out, "We believe in the Lord of the boy!" It was then said to the king, "Do you see what has happened? What you feared has taken place. By Allāh, all the people have become believers."

Angry, the king ordered large holes to be dug and huge fires to be lit in them. Then he ordered, "Whoever leaves his religion, let him go but whoever does not, throw him into the fire!"

Many people were killed because they believed in Allāh (سبحانه وتعالى). At one point, a mother was brought with a baby. She did not want to be thrown in the fire because of the baby, but her baby said to her: "Be patient, O mother! Surely you are following the truth!"[1]

Lessons

- Whenever someone wishes to learn something, they should ask questions. They should never be shy.
- Everything happens with the permission of Allāh (سبحانه وتعالى). The boy cured the ill only with the permission of Allāh (سبحانه وتعالى).
- Our trust should always be on Allah (سبحانه وتعالى). The Prophet (صلى الله عليه وسلم) said that if all the people gather to harm someone, they will not be able to do so unless Allah (سبحانه وتعالى) wills it to happen.[2]
- We should always be brave and stand up for the truth.

[1] Muslim and Aḥmad; [2] Tirmidhī

Prayer times

Ṣalāh is one of the five pillars of Islām. All Muslims perform *Ṣalāh* five times a day, every day. The picture below shows all the different times of *Ṣalāh*.

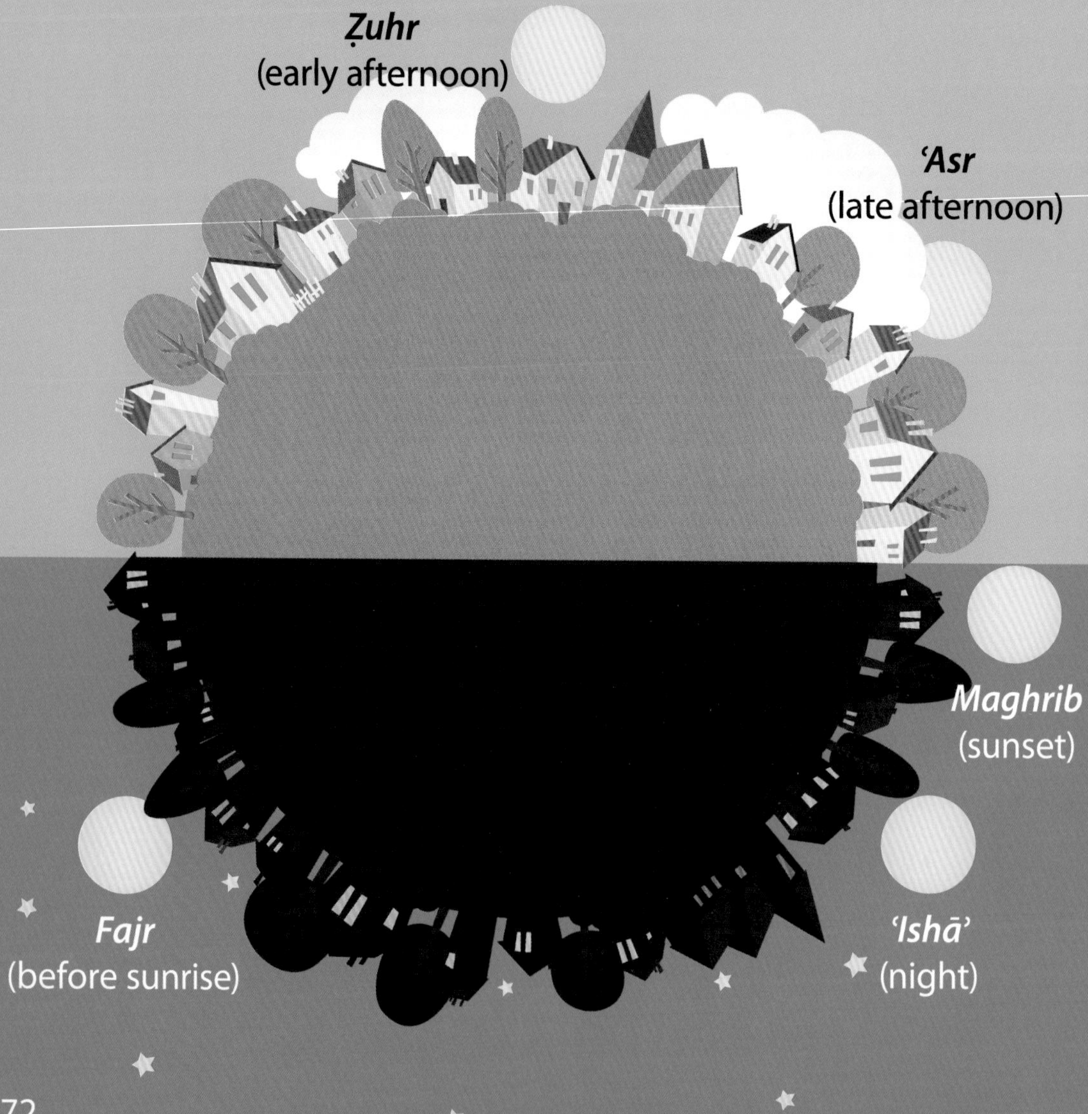

ʿAbdul Muṭṭalib

ʿAbdul Muṭṭalib was the grandfather of Prophet Muḥammad ﷺ. His name was Shaybah but he became better known by the name ʿAbdul Muṭṭalib. He was from the powerful tribe of Quraysh who lived in Makkah.

Zamzam

Early in his life, ʿAbdul Muṭṭalib took over the duty of his uncle, al-Muṭṭalib, who served water and food to those who visited the Kaʿbah. With only one son, it was very difficult for ʿAbdul Muṭṭalib to do this task. It was even harder because the well of Zamzam was lost; it had been filled with dirt for hundreds of years. He had to get water from far places which made him very tired. ʿAbdul Muṭṭalib always wished that the well of Zamzam could be found and used again.

One day, ʿAbdul Muṭṭalib saw a spirit in his dream. The spirit told him where to dig for the well of Zamzam.

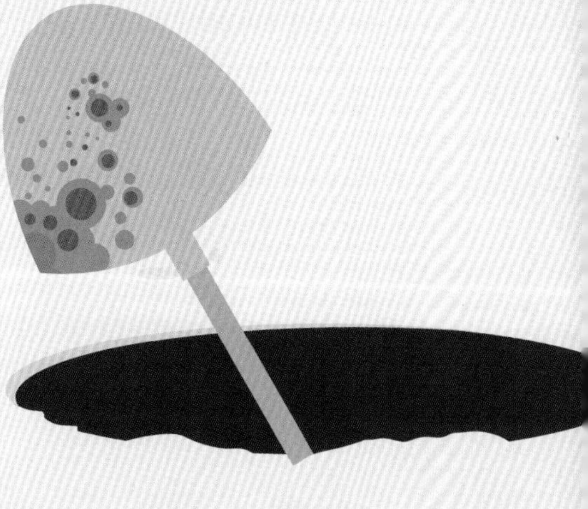

By then, ʿAbdul Muṭṭalib had a second son to help him. They dug and dug and soon water sprang out! The well of Zamzam was found, once again.

The promise

ʿAbdul Muṭṭalib's task was still difficult because he only had two sons to help him. So, he made a promise to Allāh سبحانه وتعالى that if he had ten sons, he would sacrifice one of them for Allāh سبحانه وتعالى. Soon, Allāh سبحانه وتعالى fulfilled his wish and he had ten sons.

He told his sons about his promise to Allāh سبحانه وتعالى, and they agreed to draw lots to see who would be sacrificed. ʿAbdullāh, his youngest and most beloved son, was chosen to be sacrificed. ʿAbdul Muṭṭalib being true to his promise, prepared to sacrifice ʿAbdullāh. However, people loved ʿAbdullāh very much and begged ʿAbdul Muṭṭalib to leave ʿAbdullāh and offer some wealth instead.

So they went to a wise woman in Yathrib (now known as Madīnah) to find the answer for what to give in place of ʿAbdullāh. She asked, "If a person is killed, what is the amount of money you pay?" They answered, "ten camels." She told them to go back and draw lots again but this time with two options: ʿAbdullāh's name and the other with ten camels. If ʿAbdullāh's name came up, ten more camels should be added to the original amount. Then, ʿAbdul Muṭṭalib should make *duʿāʾ* to Allāh سبحانه وتعالى and draw lots again. This should be done each time until the camels' lot was drawn.

ʿAbdullāh's name was drawn ten times. However, on the eleventh try, the camels' lot was drawn. The people of Quraysh told ʿAbdul Muṭṭalib that this was God's wish, but he disagreed and said, "By Allāh, I will not be satisfied that this is His wish until this happens three times, one after the other." So they drew lots another two times, and each time, the lot of the camels was drawn. ʿAbdul Muṭṭalib was now satisfied with the result; he sacrificed 100 camels instead of ʿAbdullāh.

ʿAbdullāh would grow up to marry Āminah, and they would have a child called Muḥammad صلى الله عليه وسلم, the final Messenger of Allah سبحانه وتعالى.

Year of the elephant

The Kaʿbah was very special to the Arabs. It became a place where Arabs from all around came to visit; the Arabs loved this place very much.

At the same time, there lived a man named Abrahah al-Ashram who ruled over Yemen. He knew very well about the fame and honour of the Kaʿbah and so decided to build a huge church in Ṣanʿāʾ, the capital of Yemen. He decorated this church with gold, silver, rubies, and other types of precious stones. It looked beautiful and amazing. Abrahah now wanted everyone to come to his church for pilgrimage and forget about the much-loved Kaʿbah.

However, Abrahah's plan did not work. People carried on going to the Kaʿbah and ignored his magnificent church; this angered him a lot. The Arabs were also angry when they heard about Abrahah's plan. They could not imagine replacing the Kaʿbah with any other building.

One day, not being able to accept Abrahah's plan, an Arab went to the church and used it as a toilet. When

Abrahah heard about this, he was furious. He promised that he would not rest until he marched to Makkah and destroyed the Kaʿbah, brick by brick.

Abrahah's army

Because Abrahah was close to the king of Abyssinia (now Ethiopia), he asked the king for help, so he could take an army and destroy the Kaʿbah. The king sent elephants for Abrahah to use. The elephants were really big and powerful, like army tanks of today.

Among the elephants, there was a special one called Maḥmūd. It was big in size and very powerful. Abrahah planned to use it like a bulldozer to destroy the Kaʿbah. Soon, Abrahah marched to Makkah with a mighty army along with the elephants.

When the Arabs heard about Abrahah's army, they all came to fight. However, any army that came in the way of Abrahah was totally destroyed!

Soon, Abrahah's army reached the borders of Makkah and stopped. Abrahah ordered his soldiers to take all the camels and other animals from the people of Makkah. Among the animals that were taken were 200 camels belonging to ʿAbdul Muṭṭalib, who was one of

the leaders of Quraysh. Abrahah then announced that he had not come to fight but had only come to destroy the Ka'bah; if anyone tried to stop him, he would kill them.

Abrahah meets 'Abdul Muṭṭalib

Meanwhile, 'Abdul Muṭṭalib went to see Abrahah. When Abrahah saw 'Abdul Muṭṭalib, he was amazed by his pleasant appearance and polite character. Abrahah, being pleased with 'Abdul Muṭṭalib, asked him what he wanted. 'Abdul Muṭṭalib replied that he wanted his camels back. When Abrahah heard this, he was surprised. He said, "I have come to destroy your beloved Ka'bah and all you want is your camels!?"

'Abdul Muṭṭalib replied, "I am the owner of the camels and concerned about them. I am not the owner of the House. The owner of the House knows

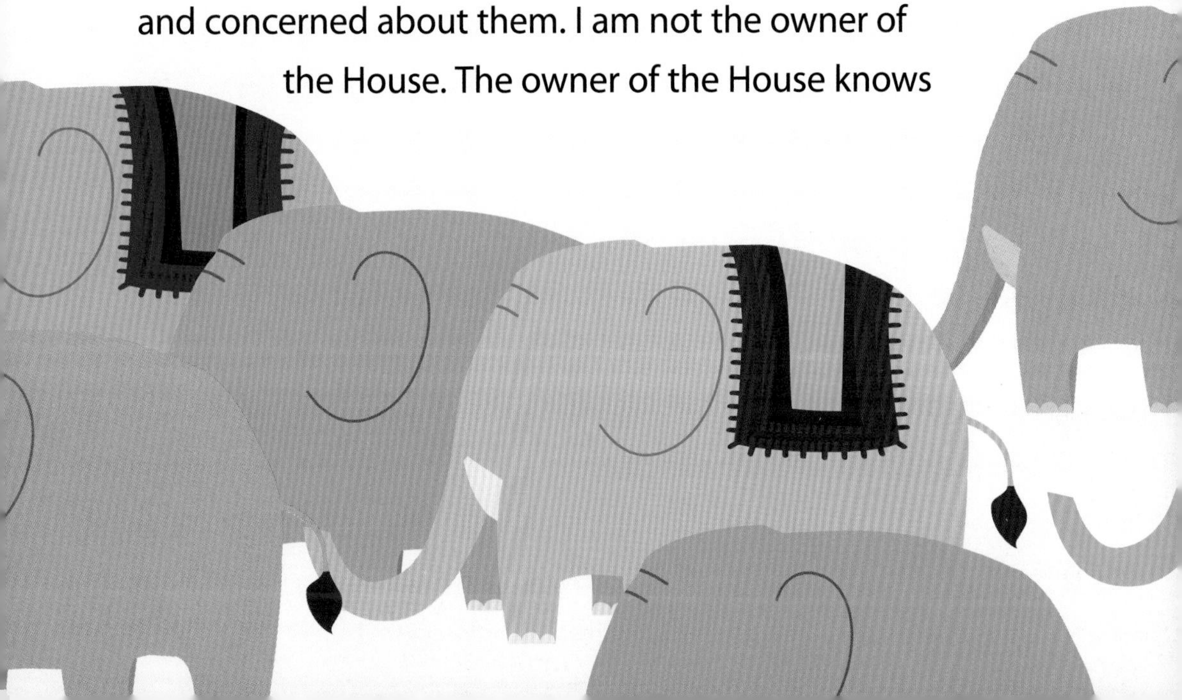

best how to protect His house." Then, 'Abdul Muṭṭalib went back to his people and told them to go to the mountains. 'Abdul Muṭṭalib and some elders stayed back, making *du'ā'* to Allah سبحانه وتعالى to protect His house.

The next morning, when Abrahah and his army wanted to enter Makkah, Maḥmūd, the big elephant, refused. It knelt down and refused to get up, even after being hit. However, if it was faced towards Yemen, it immediately got up and moved towards it.

Then, Allāh سبحانه وتعالى sent a flock of birds. Each bird carried a tiny pebble in each claw and one in its beak, and they dropped these on Abrahah's army. Despite the pebbles being small, whenever they fell on a soldier they went through him like a bullet. Very quickly, Abrahah's army was destroyed. However, Abrahah did not die in the same way. He was badly hurt and was struck with an illness. As he travelled back to Yemen, little by little, his body rotted away.

The year this event took place became known as the Year of the elephant. It was a very important year in the memory of the Arabs. For Muslims, this year is also important because it was the year in which Prophet Muḥammad صلى الله عليه وسلم was born.

Ṣalāh: two rakʿahs

A *rakʿah* is one unit of prayer. Below are the positions of prayer. Note that positions differ slightly for girls.

Practical lesson

1. Stand up straight with your hands by your side and make intention for the prayer.

2. Raise your hands up to your earlobes and then say, *"Allāhu akbar."* This is called *takbīr*.

3. Fold your hands and place them under your belly button. You then recite the following:

- *"subḥāna kallāhumma…"* (*thanā*),
- *"al-ḥamdu lillāh…"* (al-Fātiḥah),
- and any other *sūrah*.

4. Bow down (bend your back) and keep your hands on your knees. This is called *rukūʿ*. Your fingers should be spaced out. In *rukūʿ*, you say, *"Subḥāna rabbiyal ʿaẓīm."*

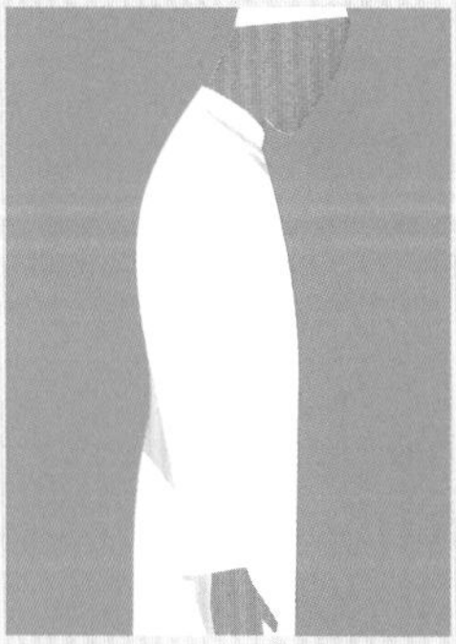

5. You stand up from *rukūʿ* with your hands by your side and then say, "*Rabbanā lakal ḥamd.*"

6. Prostrate with your feet, knees and hands on the ground. This is called *sajdah*. Your nose and forehead must also touch the floor. In *sajdah,* you say, "*Subḥāna rabbiyal aʿlā.*"

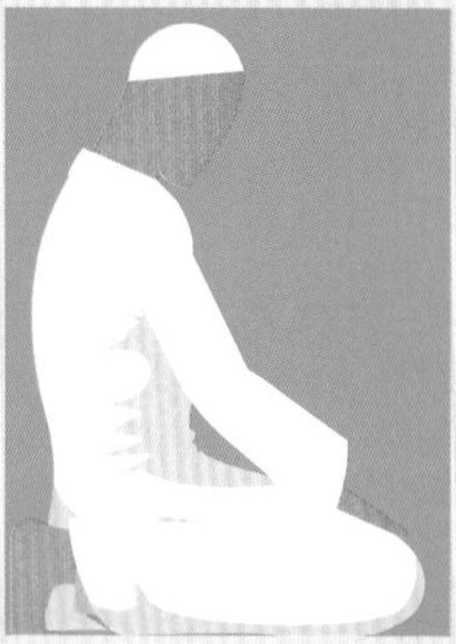

7. Sit up with your back straight, with your hands just above your knees.

8. Do *sajdah* again. You have now completed one *rakʿah* (unit).

9. After *sajdah*, perform the second *rak'ah* by repeating points 3 to 8. After *sajdah* in the second *rak'ah*, you should sit down and not stand up.

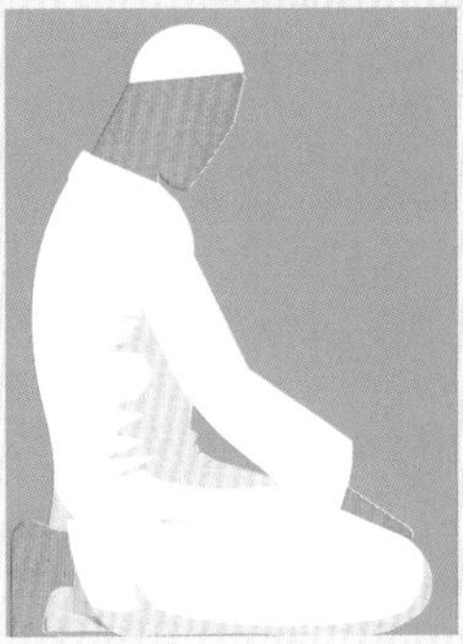

10. Sit up with your back straight, and your hands above your knees with your fingers pointing towards the *qiblah*. You should sit on your left foot and keep your right foot standing upright with the toes facing the *qiblah*. In this sitting position, you should read:

- *at-Taḥiyyāt*,
- *"allāhumma ṣalli 'alā Muḥammad…"*,
- *"allāhumma bārik 'alā Muḥammad…"*,
- and *"allāhumma innī ẓalamtu nafsī…"*

11. End the prayer by turning your head to the right and then to the left, saying, *"As-salāmu 'alaykum wa raḥmatullāh."*

The story of Ḥalīmah

It was a tradition in Makkah that babies were put into the care of families living in the desert. This was so that they grow up in a place with clean air, learn good manners and also learn to speak Arabic well.

Tribes from the desert would come to Makkah to find children to look after. They liked looking after children from rich families, hoping to get a large amount of money in return for their service.

Our beloved Prophet Muḥammad صلى الله عليه وسلم had lost his father, who died before he was born. For this reason, many of the families did not want to take Muḥammad صلى الله عليه وسلم. They thought that they would not get a good payment since he did not have a father.

Ḥalīmah رضي الله عنها adopts Muḥammad صلى الله عليه وسلم

Ḥalīmah رضي الله عنها, who was from the tribe of Sa'd, passed by Muḥammad صلى الله عليه وسلم at first and then returned. Allāh سبحانه وتعالى had put the love of Muḥammad صلى الله عليه وسلم in her heart. Āminah, the mother of the Prophet صلى الله عليه وسلم, eventually gave him to Ḥalīmah رضي الله عنها to look after.

The year in which Ḥalīmah رضي الله عنها took Muḥammad صلى الله عليه وسلم, there was very little food and water. Ḥalīmah رضي الله عنها knew that this child was a very special child because after taking Muḥammad صلى الله عليه وسلم, she noticed many blessings. On her way to Makkah, her donkey was so slow that the other women had to wait for her to catch up. However, on the way back with Muḥammad صلى الله عليه وسلم in her care, the other women were surprised at how fast her donkey was going. They asked, "Is this the same donkey you came with, O Ḥalīmah?!" Also, earlier, she did not have enough milk to give to her own child, ʿAbdullāh but now, she had enough milk for both ʿAbdullāh and Muḥammad صلى الله عليه وسلم.

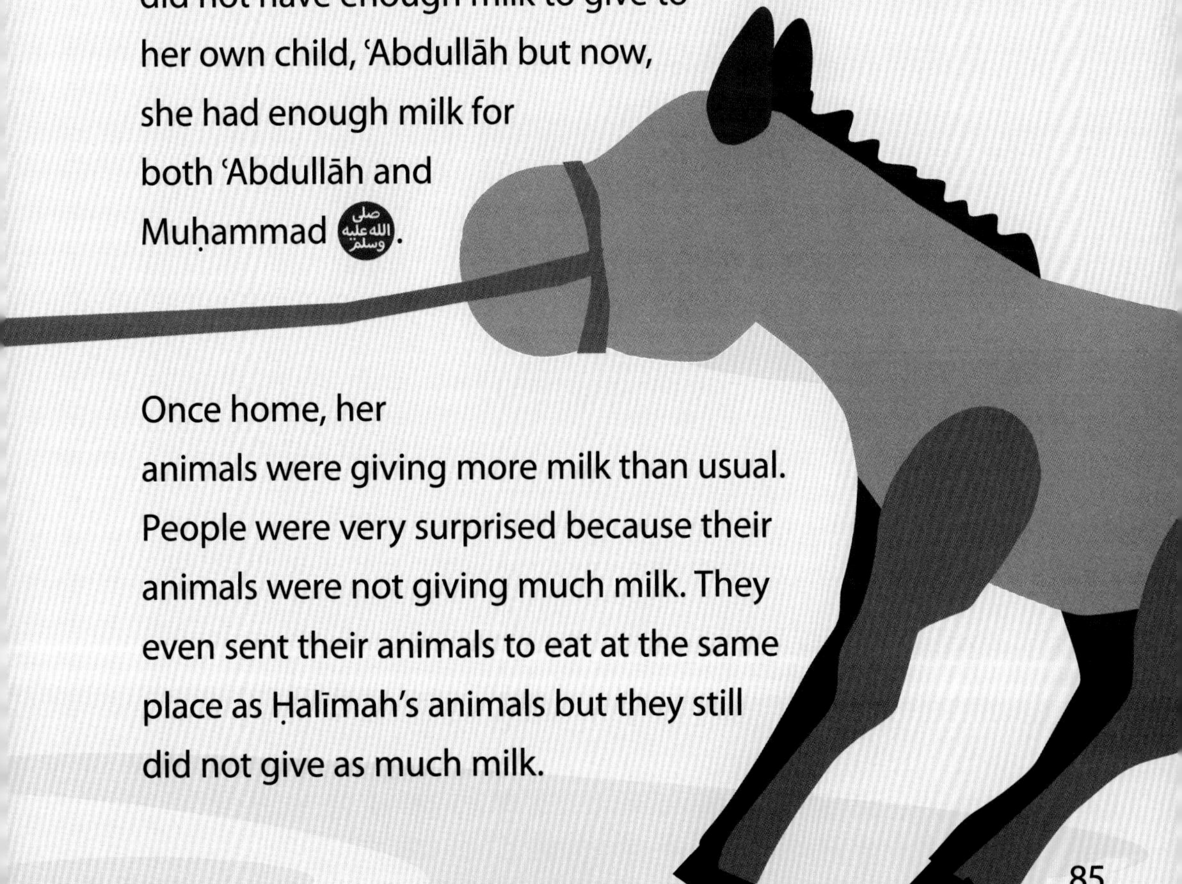

Once home, her animals were giving more milk than usual. People were very surprised because their animals were not giving much milk. They even sent their animals to eat at the same place as Ḥalīmah's animals but they still did not give as much milk.

Ḥalīmah (رضى الله عنها) returned Muḥammad (صلى الله عليه وسلم) to his mother at the age of two, as promised. However, Ḥalīmah (رضى الله عنها) begged Āminah to let her have this blessed child for longer, and Āminah agreed.

Splitting of Muḥammad's (صلى الله عليه وسلم) chest

One day, while out playing, ʿAbdullāh came running to Ḥalīmah (رضى الله عنها) and told the terrible news that Muḥammad (صلى الله عليه وسلم) had been killed. They both ran to Muḥammad (صلى الله عليه وسلم), but found him sitting down and looking very pale. Ḥalīmah (رضى الله عنها) asked Muḥammad (صلى الله عليه وسلم) what happened. He replied that two people (angels), dressed in white, came and opened his chest and washed his heart. After this, Ḥalīmah (رضى الله عنها) became worried and decided to return him back to his mother.

Muḥammad (صلى الله عليه وسلم) lived with Ḥalīmah (رضى الله عنها) for a total of four years. There, he breathed the clean air of the desert and learnt the best Arabic. He returned to his mother Āminah, at the age of four.

Sadly, his mother passed away when he was six years old. After this, he remained with his grandfather ʿAbdul Muṭṭalib. However, at the age of eight, his grandfather also passed away.

Journey to Syria

After the death of his grandfather, ʿAbdul Muṭṭalib, Muḥammad ﷺ lived with his uncle, Abū Ṭālib. Abū Ṭālib took very good care of him and always protected him. He was very kind and loved him a lot.

When Muḥammad ﷺ was 12 years old, Abū Ṭālib wanted to travel to Syria. He decided to leave Muḥammad ﷺ behind. However, Muḥammad ﷺ said to him, "O uncle! Who are you going to leave me with?" Because Abū Ṭālib loved Muḥammad ﷺ a lot , he decided to take him with him on this journey to Syria, and they set off with a group of travellers.

Baḥīrā the monk

When they arrived at a place called Buṣrā, they passed by a monastery (a place where monks live and worship God), in which there was a monk called Baḥīrā. Baḥīrā was an expert of the Bible and other holy books; he was a very knowledgeable person amongst all the Christians.

Baḥīrā never used to speak to or meet travellers that passed by. However, this time he noticed that there was a very special child with the travellers. He saw Muḥammad ﷺ from inside his monastery.

Amazed by what he saw, Baḥīrā sent for the travellers to come for a feast, inviting everyone, the young and old, so that Muḥammad ﷺ was sure to come. The travellers then took shade beneath a tree.

When they all sat together, Baḥīrā noticed that the boy was not there. He asked, "Where is the young boy that was with you?" They replied, "He is looking after our animals." Baḥīrā said, "I have only called you to this dinner because of that child." So they sent for Muḥammad ﷺ. When he arrived, there was no space for him in the shade of the tree so he sat in the sun. But a branch from the tree lowered itself to shade him.

Baḥīrā looked at him carefully. Baḥīrā asked Muḥammad ﷺ, "O young man, allow me to ask you about anything." The Prophet ﷺ replied, "Ask me about whatever you wish." Baḥīrā began asking him about his sleep and the things he does while awake.

Muḥammad ﷺ told him all that he wanted to know. Baḥīrā then looked amazed; everything this child told him matched the descriptions he had read in the holy books about the last prophet. He then looked at the seal (sign) of prophethood between his shoulder blades.

Baḥīrā then turned to the Prophet's ﷺ uncle, and asked him, "How is this child related to you?" "He is my son," Abū Ṭālib replied. "He is not your son," said Baḥīrā, "nor is his father alive." Abū Ṭālib then said, "You're right, he is my nephew." "What happened to his father?" Baḥīrā asked. "He died before he was born." "You are correct," replied Baḥīrā.

He knew this child was going to become the last prophet, so he advised his uncle: "Take him back home and take good care of him. Some people may try to harm him in Syria. This nephew of yours will be a great person one day." So Abū Ṭālib immediately took him back to Makkah. Muḥammad ﷺ lived with Abū Ṭālib who loved him very much and showed him great kindness.

Rebuilding the Ka'bah

The Ka'bah was the first house built for only the worship of Allāh سبحانه وتعالى. Built by Prophet Ibrāhīm عليهم السلام, the Ka'bah, in Makkah, was a centre of worship and pilgrimage.

Over hundreds of years, the walls of the Ka'bah became weak. There had also been a flood in Makkah when Muḥammad صلى الله عليه وسلم was young. This damaged the Ka'bah even more. The Ka'bah was now in great need of rebuilding.

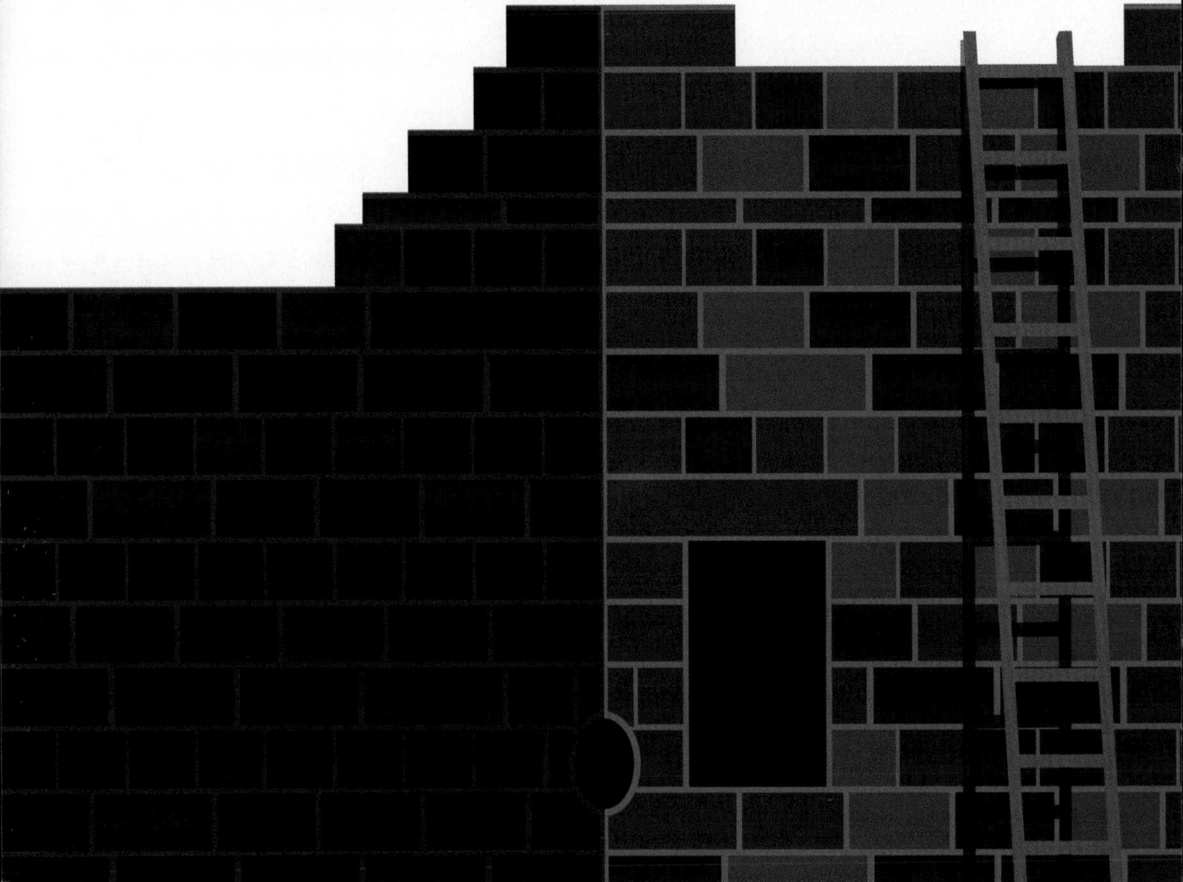

Rebuilding the Ka'bah

The Quraysh did not want to break down the Ka'bah as it was a very special place for them. So, the Quraysh and the other tribes in Makkah put together all their wealth to rebuild it. Each tribe had a special task to do. The Prophet ﷺ was 35 at the time. He helped the Quraysh rebuild the Ka'bah by carrying the bricks.

Placing of the Black Stone

One of the corners of the Ka'bah had the Black Stone. This stone was very special because it came from Jannah. During the rebuilding, when it was time to place the Black Stone, a big argument broke out between all the tribes. Each tribe wanted the special task of putting the Black Stone back in its place.

The argument became very serious; people were ready to start a war. A clan called Banū 'Abdud Dār, for instance, even promised to fight to their death. The argument continued for days, and no answer was found. The tribes called an emergency meeting, and they decided that the first person to enter the meeting place in the morning, other than them, would decide what to do.

The wisdom of Muḥammad ﷺ

The first person to enter in the morning was Prophet Muḥammad ﷺ. When they saw him, they said, "This is the trustworthy one. We are pleased with him. He is Muḥammad."

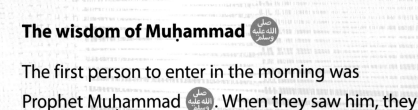

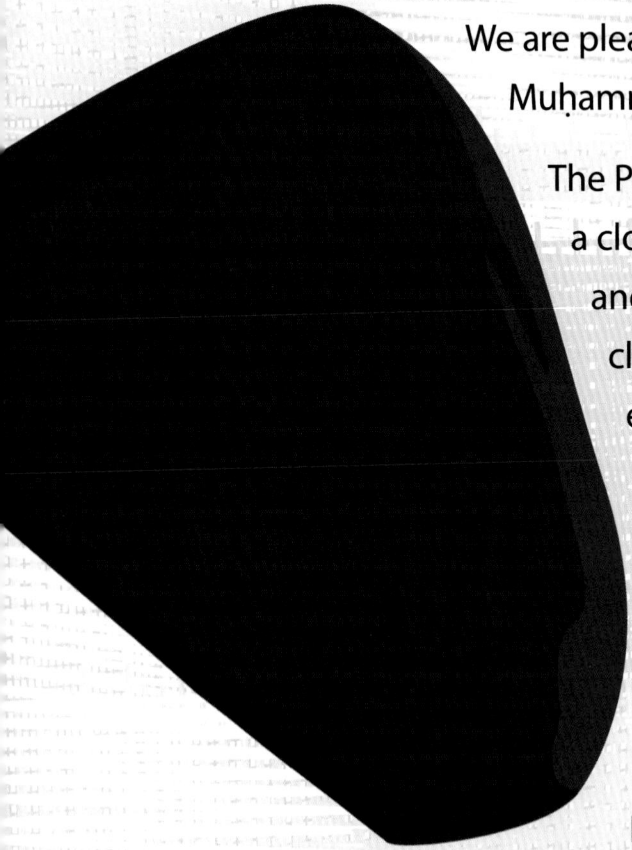

The Prophet ﷺ asked for a cloth. He took the stone and placed it on the cloth. Then, he ordered each tribe to take hold of a corner, so that they could lift the stone together. When the stone was finally brought near to the Ka'bah, the Prophet ﷺ lifted the Black Stone and put it in its place. Through his wisdom, the Prophet ﷺ solved the problem and everybody was happy.

Beginning of revelation

Signs before Prophethood

The people of Makkah were sinning openly and worshipping many gods. The Prophet ﷺ could not bear to see this around him. For this reason, he would go to mountains outside of Makkah to spend some time in a cave called Ḥirāʾ. Here, he would worship Allāh سبحانه وتعالى alone and think about how he could bring a good change amongst his people.

Closer to the Prophet ﷺ turning 40 years old, he went to this cave more often. On the way to the cave, whenever he passed by a rock or a tree they would say, "Peace be upon you, O Messenger of Allāh." The Prophet ﷺ would turn around, looking to his left and right but only to see trees and stones. He also began to see dreams that would come true the next day.

This was all to prepare the Prophet ﷺ for a great event and a very special task; the task of receiving the Qurʾān and becoming the final Prophet for all humankind.

Beginning of revelation

One day, when the Prophet ﷺ was in the cave of Ḥirāʾ, Jibrīl عليه السلام suddenly appeared. Jibrīl عليه السلام said to the Prophet ﷺ, "Read!" "I cannot read", replied the Prophet ﷺ. Jibrīl عليه السلام then took hold of the Prophet ﷺ and squeezed him tightly. After letting him go, Jibrīl عليه السلام again said, "Read!"

The Prophet ﷺ again replied, "I cannot read." Jibrīl عليه السلام grabbed him a second time, until the Prophet ﷺ could hardly breathe. After letting him go, Jibrīl عليه السلام again said, "Read!" The Prophet ﷺ yet again replied that he cannot read. Jibrīl عليه السلام for a third time did the same. Finally Jibrīl عليه السلام said:

"Read in the name of your Lord who has created; He created man from a clot of blood. Read, and your Lord is the Most Kind, Who has taught with the pen, taught man that which he did not know."

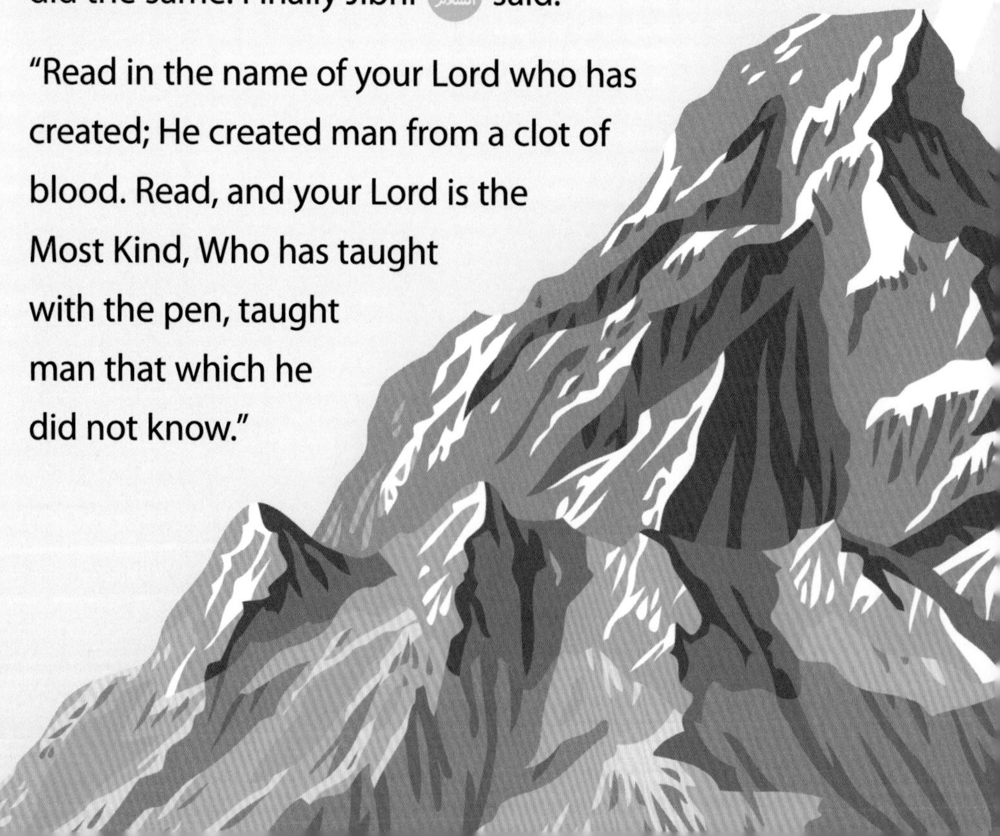

Allāh سبحانه وتعالى, through Jibrīl عليه السلام, revealed the first verses of the Qur'ān to the Prophet صلى الله عليه وسلم. This was the first day of his new task as a prophet to his people.

The Prophet صلى الله عليه وسلم also saw Jibrīl عليه السلام during the beginning of revelation. Jibrīl عليه السلام was standing on the horizon, with his feet on the ground and his shoulders in the heavens. He then spread all his wings out.

The Prophet صلى الله عليه وسلم was frightened and confused about the experiences he had. He went to his wife Khādījah رضي الله عنها, who comforted him. She then took him to her cousin Waraqah ibn Nawfal, who was a knowledgeable Christian.

Upon hearing what had happened, Waraqah ibn Nawfal said: "By the One in Whose hands is my soul, you are surely the Prophet of this *ummah* (nation). The great angel that came to Mūsā has come to you. You will surely be denied, hurt, driven out and fought against. If I witness that day, I will help Allāh's religion."

ʿUmar accepts Islām

ʿUmar was amongst the leaders of Makkah. He was respected by everyone because of his strong character. He was very tall and brave, and the Prophet ﷺ really wanted him to accept Islām. However, ʿUmar thought Islām was a problem and so, did not like the work of the Prophet ﷺ.

ʿUmar wants to harm Muḥammad ﷺ

One day, ʿUmar became really angry and went out looking for the Prophet ﷺ, waving his sword in the air. On his way to harm the Prophet ﷺ, he was asked by his cousin Nuʿaym ibn ʿAbdullāh رضي الله عنه, who was a Muslim, "Where are you going, O ʿUmar?"

"I am going to Muḥammad who has separated the Quraysh, found faults in their religion and insulted their gods; for this, I shall kill him!" replied ʿUmar.

Nuʿaym رضي الله عنه became very worried and wanted to distract ʿUmar so that he could warn the Prophet ﷺ. Nuʿaym said, "You have fooled yourself O ʿUmar. Why don't you deal with your own family first?"

‘Umar said, “What do you mean my family?”

Nu‘aym replied, “Your brother-in-law and your sister have accepted Islām and they follow Muḥammad, so deal with them first.”

‘Umar meets his sister

‘Umar headed towards his sister’s house furious with what he had heard. As ‘Umar came close to the house, he could hear something being read. ‘Umar’s sister Fāṭimah and her husband were studying the Qur’ān with a Companion called Khabbāb. When they heard the footsteps of ‘Umar near the house, Khabbāb hid in a small room whilst Fāṭimah hid the page from the Qur’ān beneath her clothes.

‘Umar burst in, and said angrily, “What is this nonsense?! I have heard that you follow Muḥammad’s religion?!” Saying this, he attacked his brother-in-law. His sister tried to stop him; in doing so she got hurt.

When ʿUmar saw his sister bleeding, he regretted what he had done. He asked them to show him the page that they were reading. She told him that he had to wash himself before he could touch the Qurʾān. ʿUmar washed himself and then began reading the first few verses of Sūrah Ṭā Hā. He was so amazed by what he read that he said, "How wonderful and beautiful these words are?!"

The Prophet's *duʿāʾ* for ʿUmar

When Khabbāb رضى الله عنه heard ʿUmar make this comment, he came out of hiding to say, "O ʿUmar, I really hope that Allāh has chosen you for the *duʿāʾ* of His Prophet. For I heard him say yesterday, 'O Allāh, strengthen Islām with Abū Ḥakam (Abū Jahl) or ʿUmar.' So come to Allāh, O Umar!"

‘Umar reaches the Prophet ﷺ

‘Umar then asked Khabbāb رضي الله عنه to take him to the Prophet ﷺ. ‘Umar, with his sword on him, followed Khabbāb رضي الله عنه to where the Prophet ﷺ was staying. ‘Umar knocked on the door and one of the Companions saw that ‘Umar was standing there with his sword. He returned to the Prophet ﷺ and said, “O Messenger of Allāh, it is ‘Umar, with his sword!”

The Prophet’s uncle Ḥamzah رضي الله عنه who was very brave, said, “Let him in; if he wants good, we will treat him well and if he wants trouble, I will kill him with his own sword!”

‘Umar accepts Islām

As he came in, the Prophet ﷺ said, “What has brought you here O ‘Umar?” ‘Umar replied, “O Messenger of Allāh, I have come to tell you that I believe in Allāh and His Messenger and in what has been revealed by Allāh.”

Hearing this, the Prophet ﷺ said, *“Allāhu akbar!”* so loudly that everyone nearby heard and knew that ‘Umar رضي الله عنه had accepted Islām.

The boycott

Islām started to spread really fast in Makkah. This was a big worry for the Quraysh who did not like Islām. In order to stop Islām spreading, they decided to write a document to stop all forms of contact with the Muslims. They announced that they would not buy or sell anything from the Muslims nor marry with them. This document was hung on the door of the Ka'bah for all to see. This whole event was known as the boycott.

The boycott was a great test for the Muslims.

Muslims were thrown out of their houses. They were forced to live in a barren valley near Makkah. The ban went on for three years.

This was an extremely difficult time for the Muslims. Food was in very short supply. Some Muslims would eat leaves because they were extremely hungry. The children could be heard crying from far, because of hunger. Despite all the hardship, Muslims did not lose trust in Allāh سبحانه وتعالى and remained strongly attached to the Prophet صلى الله عليه وسلم.

After three years, the Prophet ﷺ told his uncle, Abū Ṭālib, that the document on which they wrote the boycott had been eaten by insects.

Abū Ṭālib told the Quraysh about this. At first, they did not believe him but when they went to the Kaʿbah, they were shocked to find that it was true. Insects had eaten the whole document up except for the words, "*Bismika Allāhumma*" (In Your name, O Allāh). The Quraysh saw this as a sign from God, so, from then on, the boycott came to an end.

The ban was very hard on the Muslims. Soon after it came to an end, the Prophet's ﷺ uncle Abū Ṭālib and his wife Khadījah رضي الله عنها became very ill and passed away. The Prophet ﷺ was very upset. He called this year, the Year of Sadness.

Ṣalāh: three and four rakʿahs

Practical lesson

How to perform a three or four *rakʿah* prayer

1. Stand up straight with your hands by your side and make intention for the prayer.

2. *Takbir*: Raise your hands up to your earlobes and then say, *"Allāhu akbar."*

3. Fold your hands and place them under your belly button. You then recite the following:

- *"subḥāna kallāhumma…"* (*thanā*),
- *"al-ḥamdu lillāh…"* (al-Fātiḥah),
- and any other *sūrah*.

4. *Rukūʿ*: Bow down (bend your back) with your hands on your knees. Your fingers should be spaced out. In *rukūʿ* you should say, *"Subḥāna rabbiyal ʿaẓīm."*

5. You stand up from *rukū'* with your hands by your side and then say, *"Rabbanā lakal ḥamd."*

6. *Sajdah*: Prostrate with your feet, knees and hands on the ground. Your nose and forehead must also touch the floor. In *sajdah* you should say, *"Subḥāna rabbiyal a'lā."*

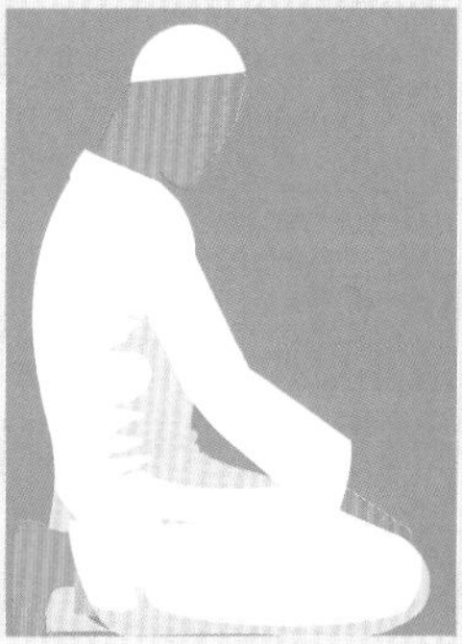

7. Sit up with your back straight, with your hands just above your knees.

8. *Sajdah*: Do *sajdah* again. You have now completed one *rak'ah* (unit).

9. After *sajdah*, perform the second *rak'ah* by repeating points 3 to 8. After *sajdah* in the second *rak'ah*, you should sit down and not stand up.

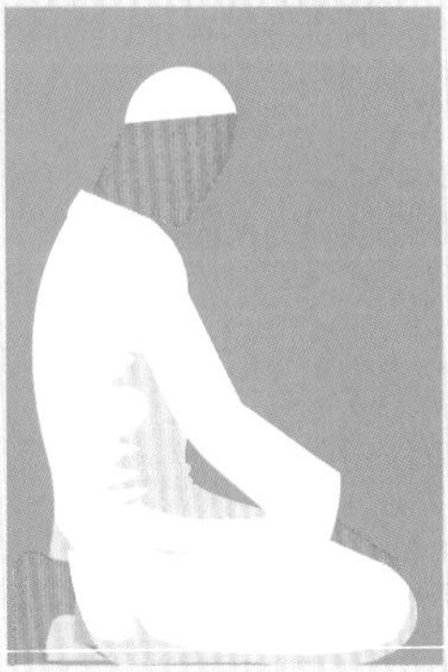

10. Sit down with your back straight, and your hands above your knees with your fingers pointing towards the *qiblah*. You should sit on your left foot and have your right foot standing upright with your toes facing the *qiblah*. In this sitting position only read *at-Taḥiyyāt*.

11. Then, perform the third *rak'ah* by repeating points 3 to 8 again. However, when you stand up read, *"al-ḥamdu lillāh…"* (al-Fātiḥah) only. No other *sūrah* should be read.

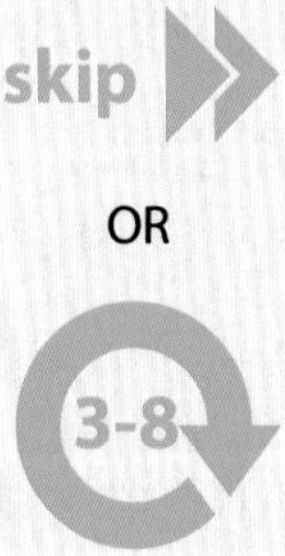

12. (Skip this step if you are performing a three *rak'ah* prayer.) If you are performing four *rak'ahs* repeat points 3 to 8 again. However, when you stand up read, *"al-ḥamdu lillāh…"* (al-Fātiḥah) only.

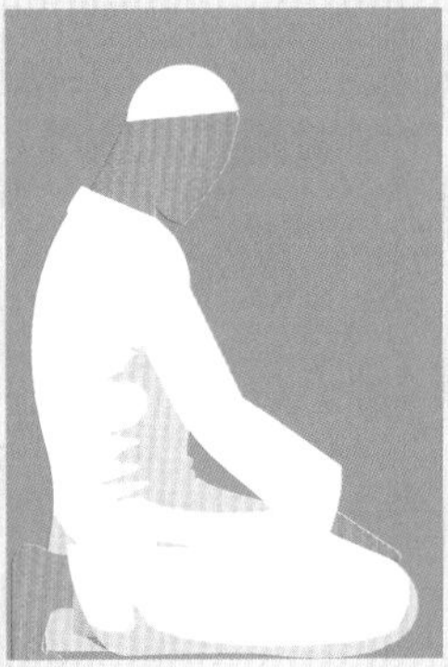

13. Sit down with your back straight, with your hands above your knees with your fingers pointing towards the *qiblah*. You should sit on your left foot and have your right foot standing upright with your toes facing the *qiblah*.

In this sitting position only read:

- *at-Taḥiyyāt*
- *"allāhumma ṣalli 'alā Muḥammad..."*
- *"allāhumma bārik 'alā Muḥammad..."*
- *"allāhumma innī ẓalamtu nafsī..."*

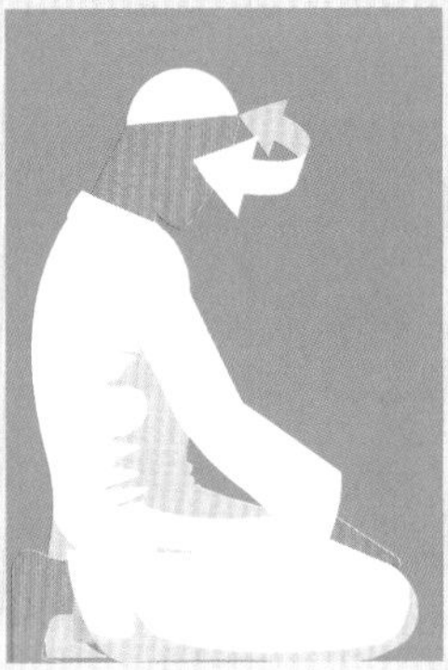

14. End the prayer by turning your head to the right, saying, *"As-salāmu 'alaykum wa raḥmatullāh."* Then turn your head to the left, saying, *"As-salāmu 'alaikum wa raḥmatullāh."*

* Note that positions differ slighly for girls.

Three and four *rak'ahs* overview

First *rak'ah*

Second *rak'ah*

Third *rak'ah*

Fourth *rak'ah*

* Skip if performing a four *rak'ah* prayer.

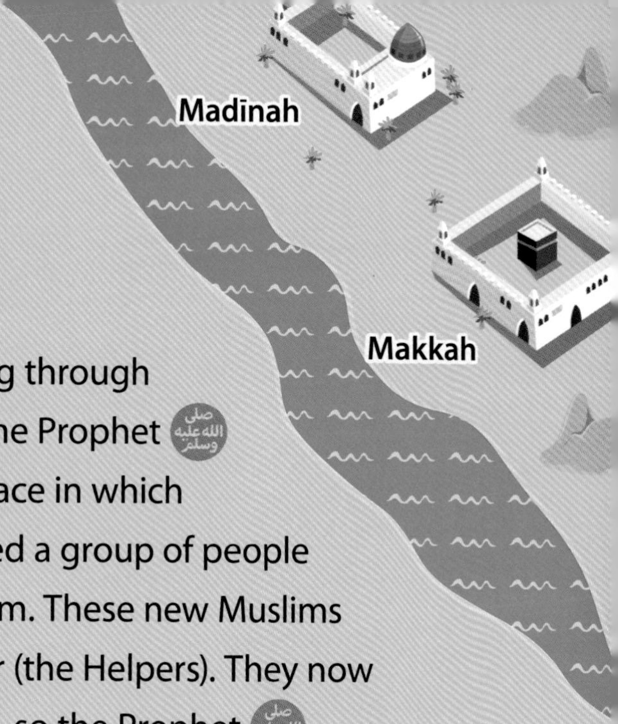

Hijrah

Because Muslims were going through great hardship in Makkah, the Prophet ﷺ began looking for a safer place in which Muslims could live. He invited a group of people from Madīnah to accept Islām. These new Muslims became known as the Anṣār (the Helpers). They now found a safe city to move to, so the Prophet ﷺ ordered all Muslims to leave Makkah for Madīnah. One by one, the Muslims left for Madīnah.

They had to leave their families, homes, and belongings. They only took with them what they could carry. The Prophet ﷺ did not leave for Makkah straight away, as he was waiting for Allāh's سبحانه وتعالى permission to do so.

When the leaders of Quraysh saw Muslims leaving Makkah for Madīnah, they became really angry. They called a meeting on how they could finally get rid of Muḥammad ﷺ and Islām once and for all. They decided that each tribe would provide one person. They would all strike the Prophet ﷺ at the same time, when he leaves. That way, no one could be blamed and the blame for his death would be divided amongst all the tribes involved. This would make it impossible for the family of the Prophet (صلى الله عليه وسلم) to fight back.

Allāh (سبحانه وتعالى) informed the Prophet (صلى الله عليه وسلم) of this plan. So he told ʿAlī (رضي الله عنه) to sleep in his bed, pretending to be him. As the people surrounded the Prophet's (صلى الله عليه وسلم) house, he opened the door and blew dust in the air. This dust went into the eyes of all the killers. As they rubbed their eyes, the Prophet (صلى الله عليه وسلم) escaped, walking right past them.

When the men from Quraysh entered the house and were about to strike, they realised that it was not Muḥammad (صلى الله عليه وسلم) but ʿAlī (رضي الله عنه). This whole event was a great embarrassment for the Quraysh.

The Prophet (صلى الله عليه وسلم) left Makkah with his friend Abū Bakr (رضي الله عنه). The Quraysh became really desperate. They knew if Muḥammad (صلى الله عليه وسلم) reached Madīnah, there would be no way to stop the spread of Islām. For this reason, they offered a reward of 100 camels for the person who finds the Prophet (صلى الله عليه وسلم). Groups of people quickly went searching for him and

Abū Bakr رضي الله عنه, so that they could catch them and win the huge prize.

The spider's web

The Quraysh followed the Prophet صلى الله عليه وسلم and Abū Bakr رضي الله عنه to a cave where they were resting. The Quraysh came right up to the opening of the cave that Abū Bakr رضي الله عنه was able to see them.

However, a miracle happened that stopped the Quraysh from entering. As the Prophet صلى الله عليه وسلم and Abū Bakr رضي الله عنه entered the cave, a spider spun a web across the entrance. This confused the Quraysh because the signs and tracks showed that the Prophet صلى الله عليه وسلم and Abū Bakr رضي الله عنه were in that cave. They said to themselves, "If anyone had entered this cave, there would not be a web across the entrance." So they all turned away.

The Muslims in Madīnah were very worried about the Prophet صلى الله عليه وسلم and Abū Bakr رضي الله عنه. When they finally arrived at Madīnah, there was great joy and celebration. It was the greatest day Madīnah had ever seen. This whole event is known as the *Hijrah*, which also marks the beginning of the Islamic calendar.

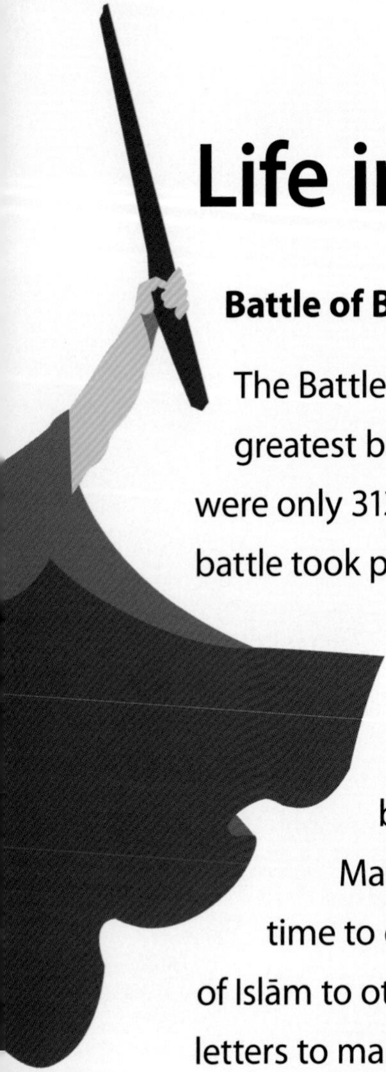

Life in Madīnah

Battle of Badr

The Battle of Badr was the first and one of the greatest battles the Muslims fought and won. There were only 313 Muslims and 1,000 non-Muslims. This battle took place in the second year after the *Hijrah*.

Inviting kings and rulers

Later, there was a peace-agreement between Muslims and non-Muslims in Makkah. This gave the Muslims plenty of time to concentrate on sending the message of Islām to other places. The Prophet صلى الله عليه وسلم sent letters to many kings, including that of the Roman and Persian Empires.

Conquering of Makkah

After the peace agreement was broken, Allāh سبحانه وتعالى ordered the Prophet صلى الله عليه وسلم to take over Makkah. When he entered Makkah, he did not kill anyone nor take revenge. Instead, he forgave everyone. This took place eight years after coming to Madīnah.

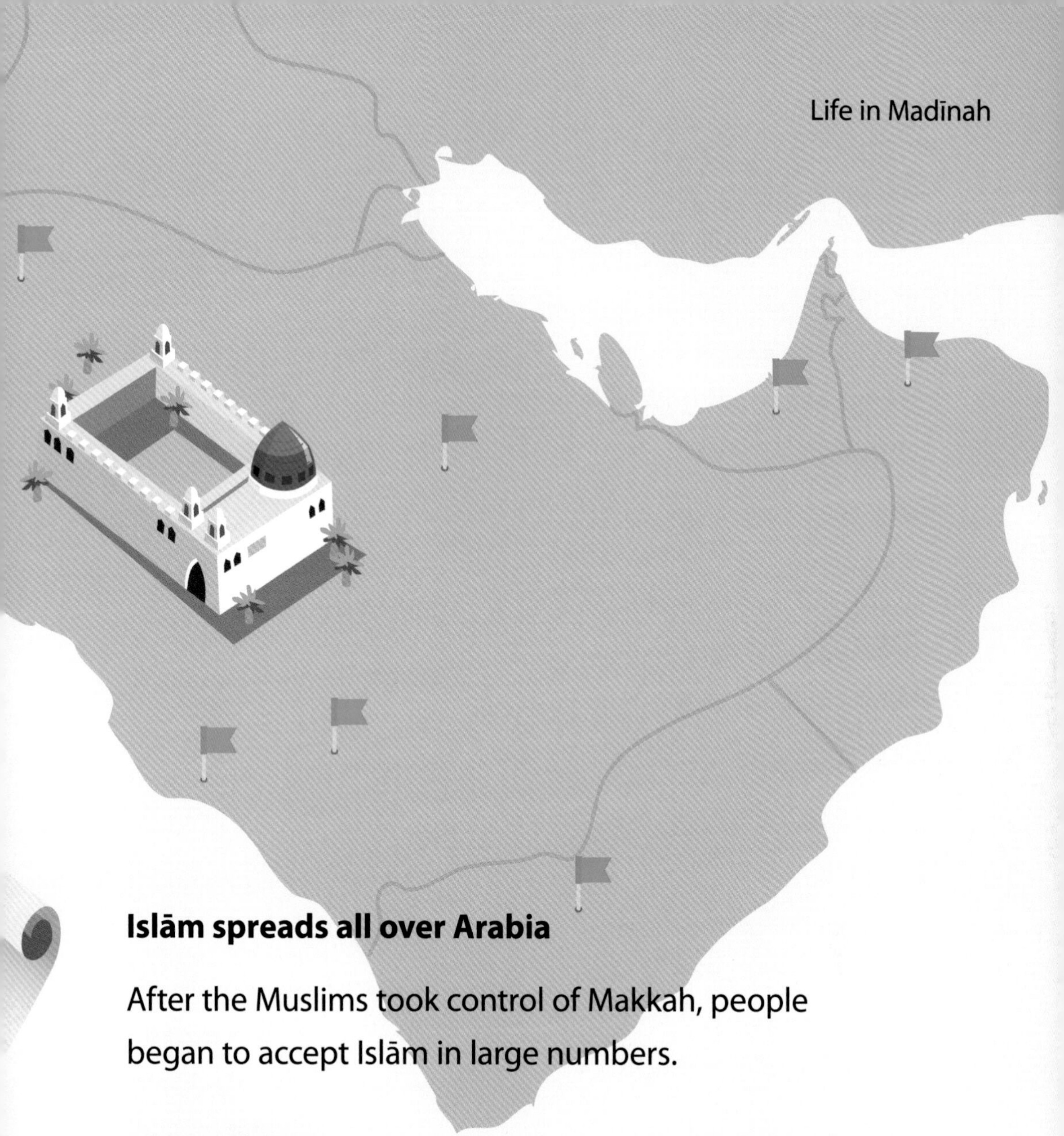

Islām spreads all over Arabia

After the Muslims took control of Makkah, people began to accept Islām in large numbers.

Farewell *Ḥajj*

In the tenth year after *Hijrah*, the Prophet ﷺ performed *Ḥajj*. This was the only *Ḥaj* the Prophet ﷺ performed. He taught his Companions how to perform *Ḥajj* and delivered a famous final speech. There were more than 100,000 Companions present on that day.

Glossary

A

***Ādāb*:** Good manners and correct behaviour, both inward and outward.

Anṣār: The Helpers; These were the residents of Madīnah who welcomed the Prophet صلى الله عليه وسلم, believed in him and helped him.

Ark: A huge ship.

B

Badr: A place near the coast, about 95 miles south of Madīnah where, in 2 AH the Battle of Baḍr took place.

Black Stone: *Ḥajarul Aswad*; The Black Stone. it is in one of the corners of the Kaʿbah.

Boycott: This was when the Quraysh abandoned the Muslims by not buying, selling or interacting with them.

D

***Duʿā*':** Praying, supplicating and asking Allāh سبحانه وتعالى for our needs.

H

Hābil: A son of Ādam عليه السلام.

***Ḥadīth*:** The sayings, actions and approvals of our beloved Prophet صلى الله عليه وسلم.

***Ḥaj*:** The annual pilgrimage to Makkah, *Ḥaj* is one of the five pillars of Islām.

***Hijrah*:** The journey of the Prophet صلى الله عليه وسلم and the Muslims when they left Makkah to settle in Madīnah.

Ḥirā': Commonly, the cave in Makkah in which angel Jibrīl عليه السلام came down to with the first verses of the Qur'ān.

I

Istinjā': Washing the private parts with water and cleaning with tissue after relieving oneself.

J

Jinn: Inhabitants of the heavens and the earth, made from smokeless fire who are usually invisible.

Jumu'ah: Friday, in which the *Jumu'ah* prayer is performed instead of *Ẓuhr*.

K

Ka'bah: The house of Allāh ﷻ in Makkah.

L

Leper: A person affected by leprosy. Leprosy is a skin disease that causes ulcers and deformation of limbs by the skin rotting away.

M

Madīnah: The city of the Prophet ﷺ previously known as Yathrib.

Makkah: The city in which the Prophet ﷺ was born and the Qur'ān was revealed.

Masjid: The place where Muslims gather to worship Allah ﷻ five times a day.

Messenger: A person sent by Allah ﷻ to guide them to the things that will please Allah ﷻ.

P

Patience: *Ṣabr*; Remaining calm at times of difficulty, bearing pain and remaining tolerant of others.

Pilgrimage: See *Ḥaj*.

Prophet: A pious male chosen and sent by Allāh ﷻ to a nation or community to guide the people and spread Allāh's ﷻ message.

Q

Qābil: A son of Ādam (عليه السلام).

***Qadar*:** Fate, destiny; The decree of Allāh (سبحانه وتعالى).

***Qiblah*:** The direction faced in prayer which is towards the Ka'bah in Makkah.

Quraysh: One of the great powerful tribes of Arabia. The Prophet Muḥammad (صلى الله عليه وسلم) was from this tribe.

R

***Rak'ah*:** A unit of the prayer consisting of a series of standing, bowing prostrations and sitting.

Ramaḍān: The month of fasting, the ninth month in the Muslim lunar calendar.

***Rukū'*:** Bowing, particularly the bowing position in prayer.

S

***Sajdah*:** The act of prostration. Placing ones forehead and hands on the ground.

Ṣan'ā': A city in Yemen.

***Ṣawm*:** Fasting; This means refraining from food and drink from dawn to sunset, particularly for the month of Ramaḍān which is one of the pillars of Islām.

Shayṭān: Satan. Evil jinn our considered to be devils, their leader being Iblīs.

***Shirk*:** To make partners with Allāh (سبحانه وتعالى) by worshipping anything other than Him, such as trees, stones, idols, and stars.

T

***Ṭahārah*:** A general term for purification, purity.

***At-Taḥiyyāt*:** The prayer recited whilst sitting after two or four units of prayer.

***Takbīr*:** Saying, *"Allāhu akbar,"* translated as, "Allāh is the greatest."

***Ṭawāf*:** Circumambulation, the ritual of going around the Kaʿbah seven times.

***Thanā*:** Praise; Usually referring to the praise recited at the beginning of prayers – *"Subḥānakallāhumma wa bi ḥamdika…"*

U

***Ummah*:** The global Muslim community.

W

***Wuḍūʿ*:** Ablution, ritual washing to be pure for prayer and reciting the Qurʾān. The face, arms and feet must be washed and the hair wiped.

Z

***Zakāh*:** An amount of charity that rich Muslims must give to poor Muslims from their wealth. *Zakāh* is one of the five pillars of Islām.

Zamzam: The well in Makkah.

***Ẓuhr*:** The midday prayer, one of the five daily prayers performed after midday.

Syllabus overview
Safar Learn about Islam Series

Book 1

Aqīdah

Who am I?
Paradise and Hell
Shahādah
The six articles of faith
The four angels and their jobs
Belief in Allāh
Belief in His angels
Belief in His books
Belief in His messengers
Belief in the Day of Judgement
All good and bad is from Allāh

Fiqh

The five pillars of Islām
Keeping clean
Using the toilet
How to do *wuḍū'*
Names of the five daily *Ṣalāh*
Times of the five daily *Ṣalāh*
Basic *Ṣalāh* positions
Fasting (*Ṣawm*)
Zakah and *ṣadaqah*
Ḥajj
Islamic months

History

Story of *Nabī* Ādam
Story of *Nabī* Nūḥ
Story of *Nabī* Ibrāhīm
Story of *Nabī* Yūnus
Story of *Nabī* Mūsā
Story of *Nabī* ʿĪsā

Sīrah

Story of *Nabī* Muḥammad

Personal/Language development

Saying *salām*
Alif to *yā* of little reminders
Classroom rules
Everyday *du'ā's*
Arabic alphabet

Book 2

Aqīdah

Names of Allāh
Jannah and Jahannam
Six articles of faith
Jibrīl teaches us religion

Fiqh

Five pillars of Islām
Basic cleanliness
When and how to perform *wuḍū'*
Actions that break *wuḍū'*
How to perform *ghusl*
Prayer times
Ṣalāh: two *rakʿahs*
Ṣalāh: three *rakʿahs*
Ṣalāh: four *rakʿahs*

History

Before Prophet Ādam
Ādam's Creation
Ādam on Earth
Prophet Nūḥ
The boy and the king

Sīrah

Abdul Muṭṭalib
Year of the elephant
The Story of Ḥalīmah
Journey to Syria
Rebuilding the Kaʿbah
Beginning of revelation
ʿUmar accepts Islām
The boycott
Hijrah
Life in Madīnah

Personal development

Bismillah
Adab in the classroom
Manners and friends
Deeds

Book 3

Aqīdah

Names of Allāh
Paradise and Hell
Angels
Books from Allāh
Prophets of Allāh
Life after death

Fiqh

Cleanliness
Manners of using the toilet
Revision of *rakʿahs*
Daily *Ṣalāh*: theoretical
Daily *Ṣalāh*: practical
Breakers of *Ṣalāh*
Ḥalāl and *ḥarām* foods

History

The story of Hābīl and Qābīl
Prophet Hud and the people of ʿĀd
The companions in the cave
Prophet Ṣālih and the people of Thamūd
Prophet Shuʿayb and the people of Madyan

Sīrah

The open invitation
Quraysh abuse the Muslims
Migration to Abyssinia
The night journey to Jerusalem and the heavens
Battle of Badr
Battle of Uḥud

Personal development

Respecting people
Manners of eating and drinking
Manners of the *masjid*
Good manners to parents and others
TV, music, games and internet
Why Muslims perform *Ṣalāh*

Book 4

Aqīdah

Names of Allāh ♡
Angels and their duties
Gardens of Paradise and fire of Hell
Signs of the Last Day
Day of Judgement
Miracles
Characteristics and duties of the prophets
Sins and *shirk* ♡ 📕
Love for the Prophet ♡ 📕

Fiqh

Najāsah
Model *wuḍū'* 🏃 ♡
Model *ghusl* 🏃
Model *tayammum* 🏃
Model *Ṣalāh* 🏃 ♡ 📕
Islamic calendar
Fasting and Ramaḍān ♡ 📕

History

Prophet Ibrāhīm ♡ 📕
Story of Dhul Qarnayn

Sīrah

Companions of the Prophet
Battle of the Trench
Ḥudaybiyyah

Personal development

Virtues of actions
Importance of *Ṣalāh*
Good character and brotherhood ♡

Book 5

Aqīdah

Names of Allāh ♡
Angels, books and messengers
From Hell to Paradise
Signs of the Last Day
Description of the Last Day
Death

Fiqh

Types of rulings
Wuḍū': *farḍ*, *sunnah* and *makrūh* ♡
Ghusl: *farḍ*, *sunnah* and *makrūh* ♡
Times of *Ṣalāh*
Forbidden and disliked prayer times
Basics of *tayammum* 🏃
Sunnah mua'kkadah and *ghayr mua'kkadah*
Witr 🏃 ♡
Farḍ acts of *Ṣalāh* 🏃 ♡
Breakers of *Ṣalāh*
Disliked acts in *Ṣalāh*
Rules and rewards of fasting ♡ 📕

History

Prophet Ayyūb
Prophet Yūnus ♡
Dāwūd and Jālūt
Prophet Dāwūd

Sīrah

Letter to Heraclius
Conquest of Makkah

Personal development

Making *Ṣalāh* part of life
Islamic dress code 🏃
Good character and sins ♡ 📕

Book 6

Aqīdah

Who is Allāh and why did He create us?
Tawḥīd and *shirk* ♡ 📕
Seeing Allāh in Jannah
Character of the Prophet

Fiqh

Rulings of *wuḍū'*
Rulings of *ghusl*
Adhān and *Iqāmah* 🏃 ♡
Ṣalāh drill 🏃 ♡
Adā and *qaḍā*
Sajdah sahw 🏃
Ṣalāh in congregation and *sutrah* 🏃
Translation of *Ṣalāh* ♡ 📕
Personal hygiene and maturity
Rulings of fasting ♡ 📕
Ḥalāl and *ḥarām* consumption ♡
Model *janāzah Ṣalāh* 🏃 ♡ 📕

History

Prophet Sulaymān
Prophet Isḥāq and Ya'qūb

Sīrah

Ḥunayn and Ṭā'if
Last days of the Prophet

Personal development

Obedience to Allāh and His Messenger
Virtues of the Qur'ān ♡ 📕
Ṣalāh: our link with Allāh
Concentration in *Ṣalāh* 🏃 ♡ 📕

🏃 Practical lesson; ♡ Overlap with the Learn by Heart Series; 📕 Overlap with the Learn Arabic Series

A FREE Support Ecosystem

Online Training

Designed to give teachers and principals the chance to **learn skills and techniques** to deliver engaging, fun and knowledge packed lessons.

Teachers Toolbox

Resources for teachers, **by teachers**.
A platform bringing together content for teachers from other teachers and institutes.

Exam Papers

We have created a set of exam papers for the Safar **Learn about Islam** series, available free for institutes registered with us.

Free Bedtime Stories

A free compilation of narrated stories available online to anybody, anywhere in the world. Available to **download online,** and as **podcasts**. Also can be used as a **supplement to your Islamic Studies lessons**.

Scan me to learn more:

NB: All these features are free to use for any organisations regardless of which syllabus you are using. We ask that you pray for us and all those who have contributed, academically and financially